Table of Contents

Grammar Made Simple
for ESL Writers

Third Edition

by

Regina A. Rochford, Ed.D.

Associate Professor,

Queensborough Community College, CUNY

Kendall Hunt
publishing company

www.kendallhunt.com
Send all inquiries to:
4050 Westmark Drive
Dubuque, IA 52004-1840

Printed in the United States of America
10 9 8 7 6 5 4 3 2 1

In memory of my daughter Rosemary

Although she never uttered a word,

she left an indelible mark on my life.

Present Tense

Read the following paragraph and underline all the present tense verbs.

Every society remembers important life events with rituals. Rituals are culturally and religiously based ceremonies that commemorate and remember major life events. Some rituals celebrate joyous events such as a marriage or the birth of a child while other rituals honor someone who has died. All rituals, however, follow cultural traditions that specify the activities people must carry out. For instance, in Chinese culture, a bride wears a red dress on her wedding day because this color symbolizes good luck, while in America, she dresses in white as a sign of purity. In contrast, European funerals, people dress in black because it represents the sorrow the family experiences when someone dies. These rules set apart each event and create a mood for the participants so that they know what behavior is acceptable for each event.

Why did the writer of this paragraph use the present tense? The writer used the present tense:

   a. to express what will be done in the future.

   b. to describe habits or routines.

   c. to state facts about rituals.

   d. b and c.

   e. a, b and c

Answer [1]

As you observed in the passage on rituals, the present tense can be used to state facts. Here are some other examples of facts in the present tense.

   a. The sky *is* blue.

   b. The sun *rises* in the east and *sets* in the west.

   c. The earth *revolves* around the sun.

   d. April showers *bring* May flowers.

   e. The professor *drinks* coffee during our class.

---

[1] If you selected choice <u>d</u>, you are correct.

The Form of the Present Tense

Examine the following examples to determine how the present tense is formed.

a. I <u>wake</u> up at six o'clock.

    I <u>prepare</u> breakfast.

    I <u>make</u> my bed.

b. You <u>waste</u> hours fixing your hair.

    You <u>need</u> to understand the importance of cultural rituals.

c. The bride <u>wears</u> a read dress.

    The father <u>walks</u> his daughter down the aisle when she <u>gets</u> married.

    A ritual <u>helps</u> people remember an important occasion.

d. My husband, daughter and I <u>entertain</u> our family during the holidays.

    We <u>take</u> a walk after supper.

e. The people at a funeral <u>wear</u> black.

    They <u>know</u> what behavior is acceptable.

    Funerals <u>allow</u> people to say goodbye to a loved one.

In the present tense, when the subject of the sentence is I, you, we, or they, the _____ form of the verb is used.

    a. infinitive

    b. simple

    c. simple form plus the letter <u>s</u>

    d. simple form plus the letters <u>ed</u>.

Answer [2]

In the present tense, when the subject of the sentence is he, she or it, the letter(s) _____ are added to the end of the simple form of the verb.

    a. ed

    b. ing

    c. s

    d. none of these.

Answer [3]

---

[2] If you selected choice <u>b</u>, you are correct.

[3] If you selected choice <u>c</u>, you are correct.

Forming the Present Tense

In the present tense, when the subject is he, she or it, add the letter *s* to the simple form of the verb. For all other subjects, use the simple form of the verb.

I <u>love</u> old movies.   We <u>love</u> to read mysteries.

You <u>love</u> to dance.

She <u>loves</u> ice cream.

He <u>loves</u> to sing.   They <u>bark</u> a lot.

It <u>loves</u> to beg for food. ◆   Dogs <u>beg</u> for food. ◆

◆ When a writer refers to an animal such as a dog or a cat, the pronoun <u>it</u> is used in the singular form, but <u>they</u> is used in the plural form.

When a present tense verb ends in the letters *sh*, *ch*, *ss*, or *x* and the subject is he, she or it, you must:

    a.   add the letters *es*, instead of the letter *s*.

    b.   add the letters *ies*.

    c.   add the letter *s*.

    d.   none of these.

Answer [4]

Observe the following examples.

    e.g.   (cash) Mary cash*es* her check at the bank.

             (toss) Monica toss*es* her books on the dining room table every night.

             (teach) She teach*es* English-as-a-Second Language.

             (fax) He fax*es* the order to his office.

---

[4] If you selected choice <u>a</u>, you are correct.

What ending is used when a present tense verb ends in the letter *y* and the subject is he, she or it?

    a. If the *y* is preceded by a vowel, add the letter *s*.

    b. If the *y* is preceded by a consonant, change the letter *y* to the letter *i* and add the letters *es*.

    c. Add the letter *s*.

    d. choice a and b.

Answer [5]

Observe the following examples.

e.g.   (carry) She carr*ies* a water bottle.

        (occupy) The child occup*ies* herself by playing computer games.

        (play) Carlo play*s* the piano at her church.

        (stay) That dog stay*s* in a kennel when his owner travels.

Verbs with Special Endings

Verbs that end in *sh*, *ch*, *ss*, or *x*

In the present tense, when a verb ends with the letters *sh*, *ch*, *ss*, or *x*, and the subject of the sentence is *he*, *she*, or *it*, add the letters *es*.

    A special machine wash*es* the windows in skyscrapers.

    The reverend preach*es* to his people during Sunday services.

    The cook mix*es* the flour, sugar and butter slowly.

    The cat hiss*es* at the dog.

Verbs that end in *y*

In the present tense, when the subject is *he*, *she*, or *it* and the verb ends in a *consonant* plus the letter *y*, change the *y* to *i* and add the letters *es*.

    I never carry a cell phone, but my husband always carr*ies* one.

    Marco and I fry our chicken, but Marisa never fr*ies* anything!

In the present tense, when the subject is *he*, *she*, or *it* and a verb ends in a *vowel* plus the letter *y*, add the letter *s*.

    My daughter stay*s* up late to chat on her computer.

    That material fray*s* after it is washed.

---

[5] If you selected choice <u>d</u>, you are correct.

Irregular Verbs in the Present Tense

In English, several verbs have irregular forms in the present tense. You must use them accurately if you want to write well. The following chart specifies these verbs and their correct forms.

Irregular Verbs in the Present Tense				
Subject	**to be** ♦	**to do**	**to have**	**to go**
I	am	do	have	go
you	are	do	have	go
he	is	does	has	goes
she	is	does	has	goes
it	is	does	has	goes
we	are	do	have	Go
they	are	do	have	Go

♦ the verb *to be* uses a different form in the negative

Controlled Practice

Complete each of the sentences with the verb in parentheses.

1. Maria, who is new parent, (worry) _____ about her infant because

    newborns (be) _____ very fragile. If a newborn (catch) _____ a

    cold, the baby can easily develop pneumonia and other serious complications.

    Therefore, infants (need) _____ to be protected from people who are ill.

2. Sanita (have) _____ few cavities because she (brush) _____ her

    teeth after every meal. In fact, as soon as she (finish) _____ eating, she (dash)

    _____ off to the bathroom to clean her teeth.

3. Paulo and Louisa (love) _____ to go to the opera, but he (enjoy)

    _____ sporting events more. Sometimes Louisa and her sister (go) _____

    to the opera without their husbands because the men (want) _____ to watch

    a baseball or basketball game.

4. When Estaban (wake) _____ up in the morning, he (stretch) _____

    his arms and (growl) _____ loudly, like a bear. After his family (eat)

    _____ breakfast, the mother (wash) _____ the dishes and (hurry)

    _____ the children off to school. Sometimes, when Tina (miss) _____

    the bus, her mother (have) _____ to drive her to school.

5. Mr. Donaldo repairs appliances for a living. He (fix) _____washing machines,

    ovens and dryers, but he (be) _____ very expensive.

6. David (coach) _____ a high school wrestling team, and he never (miss)

    _____ one of the students' wrestling matches. However, sometimes he (annoy)

    _____ his students because he (push) _____ them to get in shape

    and win.

7. My uncle (buy) _____ a foreign car every year, but he makes certain the

    manufacturer (comply) _____ with American safety standards.

8. Christina (do) _____ my taxes each year. Christina and her husband (be)

    _____ Certified Public Accounts, and they (understand) _____ the

    tax laws very well.

9. At the paint store, Alejandro, (mix) _____ the paint to the exact color the

customer (desire) _____. Before the customer (leave) _____ the

store, he (provide) _____ him/her with a sample of the paint so that

he/she (know) _____ what the color will look like.

10. That company (employ) _____ about a thousand people. Each employee (do)

_____ several different jobs so that no one person is indispensable. At my

company, we (have) _____ one specific job that is our responsibility. If I

(be) _____ absent, my work doesn't get completed. Next year, when Nina

(marry) _____ her boyfriend, her work will remain unfinished until she

(return) _____ from her honeymoon. Her absence will create serious problems

with our work flow.

11. After the baby (kiss) _____ her dolls, she (toss) _____ them out of

her crib and giggles.

12. Even though Huibing (be) _____ an adult, her mother always (accompany)

_____ her when she (go) _____ to the movies or to the mall

because she (worry) _____ about her safety.

13. It is very annoying and unsanitary when a person (touch) _____ every

piece of food on a table. In fact, when a child (reach) _____ for food, he/she

should be taught to use a serving spoon or fork to avoid handling the food.

14. Mrs. Ramos never stops talking. She really (annoy)_____ me. Sometimes she

(catch) _____ my ear when she (sit) _____ next to me on the bus.

Therefore, when I (see) _____ her entering the bus, I (hurry) _____ to

the back and (hide) _____ in a corner.

15. When a car (box) _____ in mine so that I can't pull out of the parking spot,

I am forced to wait until the driver (return) _____ because I can't move my

car without hitting his.

Practice Writing Sentences in the Present tense

With a partner, write a sentence for the verb in parentheses.

1. (relax) _____

2. (have) _____

4. (fly) _____

5. (crush) _____

6. (do) _____

7. (pray) _____

8. (catch) _____

9   (to be) _____

10. (obey) _____

11. (fry) _____

12. (miss) _____

13. (fax) _____

14. (blush) _____

15. (go) _____

The Present Tense in the Negative Form

Read each of the following sentences, and observe how the negative present tense is formed.

a. I *do not smoke*.
   I *don't smoke*.

d. In my country, we *do not drink* alcohol.
    In my country, we *don't drink* alcohol.

b. You *do not want* to swim.
   You *don't want* to swim

c. She *does not eat* pork.
   She *doesn't eat* pork.

   He *does not ride* a bike.   e. Those students *do not arrive* late.
   He *doesn't ride* a bike.   Those students *don't arrive* late.

   That canary *does not sing*.
   That canary *doesn't sing*.

The present tense is made negative by inserting:

   a.   the auxiliary verb *are* immediately after the subject. e.g. He *are not go* to work.

   b.   the contraction *don't* or *doesn't* before the simple form of the verb. e.g. I *don't like* pretzels, and he *doesn't drink* alcohol.

   c.   the auxiliary verb *do* or *does*, and the word *not* before the simple form of the verb. e.g. We *do not eat* pork, and he *does not drink* soda.

   d.   b and c

Answer [6]

Observe the following examples.

   I *am not* sure.   We *are not* mistaken.
   I *'m not* in love.   We *aren't* hungry.

   You *are not* early for class.
   You *aren't* ready yet!

   He *is not* an unkind person.
   He *isn't* late.

   She *is not* from China.   They *are not* afraid of the dark.
   She *isn't* at her desk.   They *aren't* early.

   That cat *is not* mine.
   My dog *isn't* black.

In the present tense, the verb *to be* is made negative by:

   a.   inserting the auxiliary verb *do not* or *does not* before the word *be*. e.g. He *does not be* late.

   b.   inserting the word *not* immediately after the words *am*, *is*, or *are*. e.g. We *are not* at home.

---

[6] If you selected choice <u>d</u>, you are correct.

c. using the contractions: *I'm not, you aren't, he isn't, she isn't, it isn't or they aren't.* e.g. *I'm not* happy.

d. b and c.

Answer [7]

Using the Present Tense in the Negative

The present tense is made negative by using the following rules:

e.g. I *do not like* mysteries.	We *do not have* time.
You *do not know* the password.	
Maria *does not like* to clean.	They *do not lie.*

You can also use contractions in the present tense such as in the following examples.

e.g. I *don't like* biographies.	We *don't have* time.
You *don't know* the answer.	
Elena *doesn't want* to marry him.	They *don't waste* time.

However, when the verb *to be* is negative, you need only insert the word *not* after *am, is,* or *are*.

e.g. I *am not* worried.	We *are not* children.
You *are not* correct.	
Marco *is not* unkind.	They *are not* costly.

You can also use contractions with the verb is *to be,* as in the following examples.

e.g. I*'m not* impolite.	We *aren't* children.
You *aren't* unfair.	
Cosmo *isn't* lazy.	They *aren't* liars.

Controlled Practice

Make each of the underlined present tense verbs negative.

1. We <u>work</u> every Sunday.

   _____

2. You <u>love</u> to do housework.

   _____

---

[7] If you selected choice <u>d</u>, you are correct.

3. That woman <u>is</u> my neighbor.

_____

4 That cat <u>chases</u> mice.

_____

5. Those men <u>are</u> tired from shoveling the snow.

_____

6. I <u>am</u> married to Franco. My sister is married to Davido.

_____

7. In some cultures, children <u>ask</u> their parents for permission to marry.

_____

8. Those children <u>scream</u> when they play.

_____

9. That cell phone and I-pod <u>are</u> mine.

_____

10. We <u>are</u> excited about visiting the museum.

_____

Contextualized Exercise

1. **Before reading this passage, in small groups discuss the meaning of the following new vocabulary words.**

| respirator | corpse | autopsy | post | deceased |
| dispensation | cremated | bereavement | embalm | breadwinners |

2. **Read the following passage about Muslin funeral rituals carefully, and insert the present tense wherever specified.**

Muslims (prefer) _____ to die in their own homes. They (like, not)

_____ to end their lives in hospitals or nursing homes because medical

attendants may be unfamiliar with Muslim rites. Keeping a person alive with a respirator

(be, not) _____ approved of, unless there is evidence that a reasonable quality of

life will result. When a Muslim patient (die) _____, the corpse must be ritually

11

bathed before the burial. Autopsies (be not) _____ allowed because the body is sacred, although sometimes an autopsy is performed when it is required by law.

Deceased Muslims are always buried. They (be not) _____ cremated. Moreover, the Muslim religion (require) _____ the body of the deceased to be buried as soon as possible. A Muslim's corpse (be not) _____ embalmed. Therefore, in hot weather countries for sanitary reasons, it (be) _____ very important to bury the deceased person promptly. Since the body is sacred, undertakers (transport not) _____ the body to the cemetery. Instead, it (be) _____ carried by family members in a large car or van. The people who attend the funeral (show not) _____ their heads, but cover them with caps as a sign of respect. At the funeral, the participants (form) _____ a double line facing each other and (pass) _____ the coffin on their shoulders towards the grave. It should be noted, however, that religious law (permit not) _____ Muslim women to attend burials. After the funeral, a meal is served for all those attended the funeral because the immediate family and relatives (eat not) _____ until after the funeral.

During the initial bereavement period, prayers are recited in the home of the deceased continuously. According to religious laws, a Muslim wife (leave not) _____ her home for five months after the death of her husband. If she (be) _____ pregnant, she must stay at home until she (give) _____ birth. Most Muslim women follow these rules unless they (be) _____ the breadwinners and they (receive) _____ a religious dispensation.

Forming Questions in the Present Tense

Read each of the following sentences and observe how to form questions in the present tense.

a. I eat fish everyday.

   Do you eat fish everyday?

b. You enjoy reading.

   Do *I enjoy* reading?

c. She attends college.

   Does she attend college?

d. We buy coffee in the morning.

   Do you buy coffee in the morning?

e. Those students enjoy their history class.

   Do those students enjoy their history class?

A question is formed in the present tense by:

a. first inserting the present tense of the auxiliary verb *do*.

b. next inserting the *subject* of the sentence.

c. finally by inserting the *simple form of the verb* immediately after the subject.

d. ending the sentence with a question mark.

e. all of these in this exact order.

Answer [8]

Observe how a question is formed when the verb is *to be*.

I *am* late.
Are you late?

You *are* on time today.
Am I on time today?

He *is* very funny.
Is he very funny?

She *is* angry.
Is she angry?

This watch *is* from Switzerland.
Is this watch from Switzerland?

We *are* afraid of dogs.
Are they afraid of dogs?

They *are* foolish.
Are they foolish?

---

[8] If you selected choice e, you are correct.

When the verb is _to be_, a question is formed in the present tense by:

a. inverting or switching the subject and the verb and by ending the sentence with a question mark. e.g. _Is Alex_ in class?

b. replacing the period with a question mark. e.g. They are from Spain?

c. inserting the auxiliary verb _do_ or _does_ before the subject and the simple form of the _be_. e.g. _Does Marcus be_ funny?

d. a, b and c

Answer [9]

Forming Questions in the Present Tense

A question is formed in the present tense by using the following rule:

e.g. I love swimming.	We have five cats.
Do you love swimming?	_Do you have_ five cats?
You understand the instructions.	
Do you understand the instructions?	
This lemon tastes sour.	
Does this lemon taste sour?	
Mario plays hockey.	They speak four languages.
Does Mario play hockey?	_Do they speak_ four languages?

However, when the verb is _to be_, a question is formed by inverting (switching) the subject and the verb, as in the following examples.

e.g. I am hungry.	We _are_ early.
Are you hungry?	_Are you_ early?
You _are_ in good health.	
_Am I_ in good health?	
Silvia _is_ sad.	Those diamonds _are_ real.
Is Silvia sad?	_Are those diamonds_ real?

Controlled Practice Forming Questions.

Convert each of the following sentences into a question in the present tense.

1. Rina and I work in a bakery part time.

   _____

---

[9] If you selected choice <u>a</u>, you are correct.

2.   Those dogs in that pet store need more exercise.

     _____

3.   Alicia has blond hair.

     _____

4   Mike coaches the swim team.

     _____

5.   Those children always come to school hungry.

     _____

6.   Paolo and Irina are bored.

     _____

7.   They are always prompt.

     _____

8.   The animals in the zoo smell.

     _____

9.   Those books belong to the professor.

     _____

10. Elena is my cousin.

     _____

11. I am exhausted.

     _____

12. Sara fixes breakfast every morning.

     _____

13. That chemistry book costs $550.

     _____

14. The little girl passes the ball to her friend.

     _____

15. My neighbor's dog strays onto my property every morning.

     _____

Non-Count Nouns and the Present Tense

The English language has two different types of nouns: count and non-count nouns. Count nouns describe people, places or things that can be counted such as pencils, girls, desks, chairs, etc. In contrast, non-count nouns refer to objects or concepts that cannot be counted such as milk, sugar, salt, sand, love, hatred, beauty, information. When you are writing, it is important to remember that in the present tense, non-count nouns must agree with the subject pronoun *it* (the third person singular) as in the following examples.

e.g.   Love make*s* the world go round.

Sugar *is* sweet.

Extreme hatred create*s* serious problems in the world.

That furniture cost*s* a lot of money.

Warning: non-count nouns are *never* **pluralized** in English.

e.g.   Their information~~s are~~ is inaccurate.

Uncontrolled anger~~s~~ cause*s* people to commit violent acts.

Gerunds and the Present Tense

A gerund is:

    a. an animal that is part of the rodent family.

    b. a verbal noun that ends in *ing* such as singing, dancing.

    c. an adjective such as bored or boring

    d. an adverb such the word always.

Answer [10]

A gerund can be used:

    a. as the subject of the sentence.

    b. as the verb in a sentence.

    c. to modify a preposition.

    d. none of these

Answer [11]

---

[10] If you selected choice b, you are correct.
[11] If you selected choice a, you are correct.

When you use a gerund as the subject of the sentence, the verb must agree with:

    a. the third person plural (they).

    b. the first person singular (I).

    c. the second person plural (you).

    d. the third person singular (it).

Answer [12]

Read each sentence, and observe that when the subject is a gerund, the verb agrees with the third person singular or the subject pronoun *it*. **Warning:** do not make the verb agree with a phrase that modifies the gerund.

             ↓ **modifying**
    ↓ **subject**   **phrase**   ↓ **verb**
1. Studying three languages requires time and patience.

            ↓**modifying**
    ↓ **subject**   **phrase**   ↓**verb**
2. Listening to music in the evening relaxes me.

            ↓**modifying**
    ↓ **subject**   **phrase**   ↓ **verb**
3. Educating six children costs a great deal of money these days.

Indefinite Pronouns and Subject Verb Agreement in the Present Tense
Select the list that contains indefinite pronouns.

    a. I, you, he, she, it, we, they

    b. me, you, him, her, it, us, them

    c. mine, yours, his, hers, its, ours, theirs.

    d. everyone, someone, no one, everybody, somebody, anybody, anyone, etc.

Answer [13]

When you use an indefinite pronoun as the subject of the sentence, the verb should agree with:

    a. the first person singular *I*

    b. the third person singular *he, she or it*

---

[12] If you selected choice d, you are correct.

[13] If you selected choice d, you are correct.

c. the third person plural *they*

d. the first person plural *we*.

Answer [14]

Read each sentence and observe that when the subject is an indefinite pronoun, the verb agrees with the third person singular or *it*.

indefinite
↓**pronoun** ↓ **verb**
a. Everyone know*s* about their cultural rituals.

indefinite
pronoun ↓ ↓**verb**
b. No one want*s* to argue with you.

indefinite
pronoun ↓   ↓**verb**
c. Somebody always get*s* in trouble.

Non-Count Nouns in the Present Tense

Non-count nouns refer to objects or concepts that can not be counted such as information, milk, coffee, honesty. When the subject of a sentence is a non-count noun, the present tense verb must agree with the third person singular (it).

e.g.   Her information is accurate.
    Caffeine enlivens people.

Gerunds

Gerunds are nouns that end in *ing* such as *talking, studying, working*. When the subject of a sentence is a gerund, the verb must agree with the third person singular (it).

e.g.   *Writing* a good novel takes lots of creative energy.
    Taking standardized tests makes people anxious.

Indefinite Pronouns

When the subject of the sentence is an indefinite pronoun such as everyone, someone, nobody, etc, the subject of the sentence must agree with the third person singular (it).

e.g.   *No one* likes a complainer.
    Everyone loves Raimondo.
    Somebody uses my computer at night.

---

[14] If you selected choice <u>b</u>, you are correct.

18

Controlled Exercise

Complete each sentence with the correct form of the verb in the present tense.

1. Everyone in this course (come) _____ from a foreign country, but no one (be) _____ from Argentina.

2. Watching television programs (be not) _____ a good way to learn a second language. Learning a language (require) _____ interaction with other people to develop fluency. Everybody also (need) _____ to listen, speak, read and write to communicate effectively in a new language. Clearly, viewing television programs (teach not) _____ reading and writing.

3. These days the most current and up-to-date information (be) _____ available on-line. In fact, surfing the Internet (be) _____ the preferred method of research among many people. However, they also use the Internet to make plans and to socialize. A recent survey in a college indicated that no one (use) _____ the telephone to communicate regularly. Instead, they communicate through text messages or instant messages because these methods (permit) _____ them to speak quickly, and e-mail (provide) _____ faster communication, too. In addition, chatting on line with many friends (allow) _____ teenagers to engage in more social interaction without leaving their homes.

4. Cheese (come) _____ in several different varieties and colors, but fresh milk (be) _____ usually white. Although sugar (be) _____ usually white or brown, salt (be) _____ always white.

5. American literature (contain) _____ many stories about how the United States evolved from a small group of colonies into a large nation.

6. The noise outside of that classroom (disrupt) _____ the students so that taking lecture notes (be, not) _____ easy.

7. The health of unborn babies (concern) _____ most obstetricians and expectant parents.

8. Knowledge (be) _____ power, but ignorance (be) _____ bliss.

9. Air pollution (endanger) _____ the health of human beings because people (inhale) _____ impure poisonous air. Dirty air also (damage) _____ plants.

10. Music (help) _____ people relax, although listening to loud songs (make) _____ some people nervous.

11. Pork (have) _____ to be cooked thoroughly to avoid contracting diseases.

12. Soda (contain) _____ sugar and many calories, but water (be) _____ healthy and calorie free.

13. Drinking a lot of beer and wine (result) _____ in weight gain and high blood pressure.

14. Someone (leave) _____ anonymous messages on my phone every night. I wonder why no one ever (state) _____ his/her name.

15. Everybody (love) _____ somebody, and everyone (need) _____ someone to care about.

Controlled Error Analysis

Read each of the following statements and correct any mistakes in the use of the present tense.

1. Because Americans eat so much fast food, obesity among children increase every year.

2. A college education not only teaches students skills, but prepare them to obtain better employment.

3. Many people in our neighborhood celebrates Chinese New Years.

4. Fifty percent doesn't want to have a parade.

5. In many cultures, arranged marriages is part of a greater system of beliefs.

6. Arranged marriages force two innocent strangers into a life time commitment.

7. My friends get nervous when someone mention that traumatic event.

8. When an emergency is happen, an ambulance will arrive within five minutes.

9. The family are offer the bride a big red apple to wish her good luck in her marriage.

10. Teaching children good manners are very important because youngsters must know how to behave when they grows up.

Context Error Analysis

Read each of the following paragraph and correct any mistakes in the use of the present tense.

In many cultures, a young person don't select his/her own spouse. Instead, his/her parents are arrange a marriage. Arranged marriages guarantees that a child has a respectable mate. In China, when the parents select a husband for their daughter, their decision is based on practical aspects, such as honesty, diligence, and humility. Chinese parents believes if a man have good, moral values, their daughter will have a happy and successful marriage. In contrast, in the United States, when young people are fall in love, their parents doesn't have control over their decision to wed. Therefore, the American divorce rate increase annually. This occur because when some Americans focus on money and physical attractiveness. However, once the physical beauty fade and problems are appear, many of these marriages fail. On the other hand, arranged marriages are very successful, because they are logical and objective. If a couple have similar backgrounds, interests, and personalities, this foundation form a solid long-lasting relationship, which will grow into love as the couple are mature. This is why couples that have arranged marriages have fewer divorces.

Response Writing

Write a paragraph explaining why you agree or disagree with arranged marriages.

Practice Writing.

Select one of the following writing assignments.

1. Select a ritual from your culture and describe it using the present tense and all the subject pronouns: *I, you, he, she, it, we,* and *they.* This ritual could include birth, death, marriage, religious events, birthdays, anniversaries, graduations, holidays, or another special season, etc.

2. Write a composition describing your favorite or least favorite holiday, and be certain to explain what you like or dislike about this tradition by using the present tense and all the subject pronouns: *I, you, he, she, it, we,* and *they.*

The Past Tense

The goal of this chapter is to instruct you in the form and use of the past tense so that you will know exactly when it is necessary to use the past tense.

The Meaning of the Past Tense: The Past versus the Present Tense

With a partner, read the following passage and identify whether the underlined verbs are in the simple present or past tense.

1.   Although young people <u>heal</u> faster than older people, when it <u>comes</u> to coping with chronic, constant pain, the opposite <u>occurs</u>. A recent study <u>examined</u> approximately 6,000 patients who <u>received</u> pain reduction treatment, and the researchers <u>determined</u> that the patients who <u>were</u> over fifty years of age <u>endured</u> the pain better than the younger people.

2.   To measure the impact of the pain on the participants' lives, the researchers <u>asked</u> the subjects to describe the intensity of the pain and the level of their disability. The patients were also asked how well they <u>slept</u> and if they <u>used</u> alcohol or drugs to reduce the pain. A comparison of the two groups <u>concluded</u> that the younger patients <u>claimed</u> to have more pain.

3.   The researchers <u>believe</u> there could be several explanations for these results. They <u>think</u> these results may occur because the younger adults <u>have</u> more work and family demands than the older people. However, this research <u>suggests</u> the level of pain that a person <u>experiences</u> may be attitudinal.

Analysis of Tense Usage in this Passage

1. **In paragraph 1 of this passage, the first sentence is written in the present tense because the author:**

   a. likes the way it sounds.

   b. doesn't know that it is wrong to switch tenses.

c. is stating a fact.

d. a and b

Answer [1]

2. **The second sentence of this passage uses the past tense because:**

   a. the study has already been completed.

   b. the passage is describing an action that occurred in the past.

   c. it is describing an activity that was occurring in the past.

   d. a and b

Answer [2]

3. **The third paragraph switches back to the present tense because:**

   a. the author wants to state a current belief or a theory.

   b. the passage is describing an action that will occur in the future.

   c. the passage is describing an activity that is in progress right now.

   d. a and b

Answer [3]

Using the Past Tense

The past tense expresses an activity that has already occurred and is completed.

e.g.   Two groups of people **participated** in the experiment. One group **contained** young people while the other group **consisted** of senior citizens.

The past and present tenses should not be confused because the present tense expresses facts or habitual actions, not past events.

e.g.   Physicians **acknowledge** that young people **heal** faster than the elderly.

---

[1] If you selected choice c, you are correct.
[2] If you selected choice d, you are correct.
[3] If you selected choice a, you are correct.

The Form of the Past Tense

Examine the following examples to determine how the past tense is formed.

I <u>yelled</u> for help.

You <u>examined</u> the young participants.

The researcher <u>concluded</u> that young people <u>experienced</u> more pain than the elderly.

The professor and I <u>interviewed</u> 6,000 patients.

The patients <u>received</u> pain reduction treatment.

The past tense is formed by adding the letter(s) _____ to the verb.

    a. s

    b. es

    c. d or ed

    d. a and b.

Answer [4]

What ending is used when a regular past tense verb ends in the letter _y_?

    a. If the _y_ is preceded by a vowel, add the letters _ed_, such as _played_ or _stayed._

    b. If the _y_ is preceded by a consonant, change the letter _y_ to the letter _i_ and add the letters _ed_ such as _worried_ or _dried._

    c. Add the letter d.

    d. choice a and b.

Answer [5]

Observe the following examples.

e.g.   (worry) Sadaf worr**ied** that she would fail her exam.

        (occupy) The game occup**ied** the children all night.

        (employ) The Yankees employ**ed** the highest paid baseball players.

        (annoy) That man annoy**ed** everyone on the bus by shouting at the bus driver.

---

[4] If you selected choice <u>c</u>, you are correct.

[5] If you selected choice <u>d</u>, you are correct.

Forming the Past Tense

The past tense is formed by:

1. **adding the letter *ed* if the verb ends in a consonant.**

   e.g. I <u>talked</u> to Monique.
   We <u>fixed</u> the dish washer.

2. **adding the letter *d* if the verb ends in the letter *e*.**

   e.g. She <u>received</u> the guests.
   The dog <u>chased</u> the birds in the yard.

3. **changing the letter *y* to *i* and adding *ed*, if the letter *y* is preceded by a *consonant*. ♦**

   e.g. He <u>fried</u> the fish.
   They <u>carried</u> two bags of groceries home.

4. **adding the letters *ed*, if the verb ends in the letter *y* and is preceded by a *vowel* ♦**

   e.g. That company <u>employed</u> five hundred people.
   The children <u>played</u> tag.

♦ if the verb is not irregular

Controlled Practice

Complete each of the following sentences with the past tense.

1. When I was in elementary school, I (travel) _____ to school by bus.

2. Alberta (attend) _____ college part time while she (work) _____ full time.

3. Ciara (love) _____ to write short stories as a child.

4. Mario and Clara (bake) _____ cookies for the holiday party.

5. In last year's study, the researchers (believe) _____ the young people would experience less pain than the older participants.

6. It (rain) _____ everyday when we were on vacation.

7. That dog (stray) _____ outside the house when the child (open) _____ the gate.

8. Marcela and Pietro (employ) _____ thirty-five people when they
    (own) _____ the pizzeria.

9. Xia (like) _____ to drive to work at night when he (live) _____ in the
    city.

10. It (snow) _____ several inches yesterday.

11. The woman (dash) _____ down the aisle to get the free bag of sugar.

12. The woman (patch) _____ up the tear on her son's pants.

13. Maria (marry) _____ Lucas last year.

14. The woman (dry) _____ her hair with a towel.

15. They (yell) _____ for help when the elevator (stop) _____ between
    floors.

Practice Writing Sentences in the Past tense

With a partner, using the list provided below, write a paragraph that contains at least five
sentences about your past life in your homeland.

cook	learn	listen	clean	imagine	turn on
guess	cry	laugh	select	annoy	hire
dance	open	close	enjoy	live	delay
work	live	marry	die	obey	study

_____

_____

_____

_____

_____

_____

Irregular Verbs in the Past Tense

In English, many verbs have irregular forms in the past tense. To be a good writer, you must spell and use irregular verbs accurately. To assist you in meeting these goals, a complete list of the most common irregular verbs in English is provided in Appendix A.

Frequent Errors in the Use of Irregular Past Tense Verbs

This section reviews some common errors students make in using irregular past tense verbs.

- Was versus Were

  When using the verb *to be* in the past tense, the subject must agree with the verb. For instance, if the subject is singular (I, he, she, or it), use the word *was*, but if it is plural (you, we or they), use *were*.

  e.g.   Angelo *was* in his office before eight o'clock this morning.

          His English *was* difficult to understand.

          We *were* unable to call you.

          You *were* ready to leave when I arrived.

- Bought versus Brought

  The word *bought* is the past tense of the verb *buy*, and *brought* is the past tense of bring. Note how these words are used in the following examples.

  (bring: past tense) Frank <u>*brought*</u> a cake to his mother's house.

  (buy: past tense) I <u>*bought*</u> a new car last year.

- Fell versus Felt

  The past tense of the word *feel* is *felt*. *Fell* is the past tense of the verb *fall*. Observe the following examples.

  (feel: past tense) Maria left the office early because she <u>*felt*</u> sick.

  (fall: past tense) The child tripped on the rock and <u>*fell*</u> down.

- Thought versus Through versus Though

  The word *thought* is the past tense of the verb *think*, and can be a noun, too. However, the word *through* is a preposition.

  Finally, *though* is a subordinating conjunction that creates a dependent adverbial clause. Note the use of these words in the following examples.

28

(think: past tense verb) She *thought* about him everyday while he was away.

(thought: noun) Her *thoughts* on the subject were never discussed.

(through: preposition) The child ran *through* the door screaming.

(though: subordinating conjunction) *Though* Marcela loved Enrique dearly, she was still disappointed in his behavior.

- Taught versus Thought

The word *taught* is the past tense of the verb *teach*. However, the word *thought* is the past tense of the verb *think,* and as mentioned previously, the word *thought* can also function as a noun. Observe the following examples.

(teach: past tense) She *taught* English for thirty years.

(think: past tense verb) He *thought* he knew the answer.

(thought: noun) Her *thoughts* were quite unclear and confusing.

- Threw versus Through

The word *threw* is the past tense of the verb throw. However, as mentioned previously, the word *through* is a preposition. Observe the following examples.

(throw: past tense verb) Martinez *threw* the ball out the stadium.

(through: preposition) We walked *through* a long hallway in the cathedral.

- Send versus Sent

The word *send* is the present tense and the simple form of the verb. However, *sent* is the past tense and the past participle of the verb.

(send: present tense) We *send* Alicia flowers every year on her birthday.

(sent: past tense) Last year he *sent* her twenty-four yellow roses.

- Build versus Built

The word *build* is the present tense and the simple form of the verb; however, *built* is the past tense and the past participle.

(build: present tense) Those men *build* houses for a living.

(built: past tense) Mr. Trump *built* Trump Towers.

- Catch and Caught

When using the past tense, you may be tempted to add the letters *ed* on the end of the word *catch*; however, this form is incorrect. The past tense of the word *catch* is *caught*.

(catch: present tense) They *catch* the ball during the baseball game.

(caught: past tense) The child *caught* pneumonia.

- Meet versus Met

Many writers confuse the present tense verb *meet* with the past tense verb *met*. One trick that assists writers in selecting the correct word is to remember that the past tense verb *met* rhymes with words such as *bet, get, jet, let, net, pet, set,* and *wet*, while the present tense verb form, *meet*, rhymes with *beet*, and *feet*.

(meet: present tense) My class *meets* at 10 o'clock every morning.

(met: past tense) I *met* my husband at work.

- Went versus When

Because the words *when* and *went* are close in pronunciation, many students use the wrong word when they write. The past tense of the verb *go* is *went*. On the other hand, the word *when* is used to ask a question of time, or it can also function as a relative pronoun in a noun clause.

(went: past tense of go) She *went* to the doctor's yesterday.

(when: question word) *When* is she getting married?

(when: relative pronoun) I asked her *when* the party would begin.

Controlled Practice

Complete each sentence with the correct form of the past tense. If you are uncertain of the form or spelling, refer to Appendix A for assistance.

1. Marisa (draw) _____ two pictures and (sell) _____ them for $100 each.

2. When Alicia (catch) _____ the flu, she (feel) _____ very sick for two weeks.

3. When Chang (fall) _____ off the bike, he (break) _____ his leg.

4. Malek (teach) _____ his sister to drive a car.

5. When Soon (get) _____ on the bus, she (have) _____ to stand because it (be) _____ crowded.

6. When the door bell (ring) _____, I (send) _____ my daughter to answer it.

7. The robber (flee) _____ the store quickly.

8. Everyone was shocked, when the little boy (throw) _____ the ball across the field.

9. Because Augusto (build) _____ his own house, he (pay) _____ a lot less money than we (do) _____.

10. The child (fall) _____ when she was running in the park.

11. When I (feed) _____ the children, they (sit) _____ at the kitchen table.

12. Peter (wake) _____ up when he (hear) _____ someone enter the house.

13. She (pay) _____ her cellular phone bill late because she (have) _____ so many additional charges for text messages.

14. Angelo (take) _____ so much time deciding if he should marry Louisa that she (get) _____ impatient and (marry) _____ someone else.

15. I (write) _____ a thank you note to my grandmother after she (send) _____ me a gift for my birthday.

Practice in Context

Read the following information about pain reduction carefully. Then determine if you should use the present or the past tense to complete each sentence.

Several physicians have discovered that when people (experience) _____ lower back pain that psychological treatments (have)_____ a small, but real impact on the intensity of the pain. In addition, these treatments sometimes (improve) _____ the patients quality of life.

A few years ago, several doctors (review) _____ twenty-two studies that tested the effectiveness of psychological treatments for chronic lower back pain. They (compare) _____ these results to control groups that received no treatment or medications. The therapy (include) _____ cognitive behavioral treatment, biofeedback, and relaxation techniques.

After statistical analyses were conducted, the investigators (conclude) _____ that these treatments (have) _____ positive impacts on the intensity of the pain and the quality of life. Cognitive behavioral therapy, biofeedback and relaxation techniques (evidence) _____ the greatest reduction in pain. Moreover, self-regulatory therapies (reduce) _____ the depression associated with back pain.

This study (provide) _____ the most compelling proof that pychological

interventions can impact how people (perceive) _____ pain.

Practice Writing

Write a paragraph describing a time you or someone you know had difficulty sleeping, studying or concentrating because of pain or anxiety. Describe what caused the problem and how it was resolved.

Negation: Making the Past Tense Negative

Read each of the following sentences and observe how the past tense is made negative.

I *did not cheat* on the test.
I *didn't cheat* on the test.

You *did not understand* the question.
You *didn't understand* the question.

She *did not write* the note.
She *didn't write* the note.

He *did not like* soda.
He *didn't like* soda.

The child *did not miss* the bus.
The child *didn't miss* the bus.

We *did not lie* to her mother.
We *didn't lie* to her mother

The teachers *did not grade* their own students' papers.
The teachers *didn't grade* their own students' papers.

The past tense is made negative by:

a. inserting the auxiliary verb *did* immediately after the subject, the word *not*, and the *simple form of the verb*. e.g. *Maria did not eat.*

b. inserting the word *did not* before the subject of the sentence, and then the simple form of the verb. e.g. *Did not Maria eat.*

c. inserting the auxiliary verb *were* immediately after the subject and then the word *not*. e.g. *Maria were not eat.*

d. inserting the contraction *didn't* immediately after the subject and before the *simple form of the verb*. e.g. *Sana didn't complain.*

e. a and d.

Answer [6]

Read each of the following sentences and observe how a past tense is made negative when the verb is *to be*.

Ana *was* at school.
Ana *was not* at school.
Ana *wasn't* at school.

You *were* in the pool.
You *were not* in the pool.
You *weren't* in the pool

She *was* angry at me.
She *was not* angry at me.
She *wasn't* angry at me.

He *was* very impatient.
He *was not* very impatient.
He *wasn't* very impatient.

The bird *was* bright red.
The bird *was not* bright red.
The bird *wasn't* bright red.

We *were* certain of the answer.
You *were not* certain of the answer.
You *weren't* certain of the answer.

The teenagers *were* at the dance.
The teenagers *were not* at the dance.
The teenagers *weren't* at the dance.

In the past tense, the verb *to be* is made negative by:

a. inserting the word *not* immediately after the words *was* or *were*. e.g. *She was not sick*.

b. using the contraction *wasn't* or *weren't* after the subject. e.g. *Maria wasn't happy*.

c. inserting the word *not* before the words *to be*. e.g. *Silvia not be absent*.

d. a and b.

Answer [7]

---

[6] If you selected choice <u>e</u>, you are correct.
[7] If you selected choice <u>d</u>, you are correct.

Using the Past Tense in the Negative

The past tense is made negative by using the following rule:

e.g.   I *did not know* her husband.   We *did not have* a pet.
You *did not have* any money.
Maria *did not speak* to him.   They *did not love* her.

You can also use contractions in the past tense such as in the following examples.

e.g.   I *didn't speak to* his wife.   We *didn't have* a pet.
You *didn't know* the number.
Maria *didn't notice* him.   They *didn't like* the cat.

However, when the verb *to be* is negative, only insert the word *not* after *was*, or *were*.

e.g.   I *was not* at work last night.   We *were not* satisfied.
You *were not* alert.
Alana *was not* friendly.   They *were not* expensive.

You can also use contractions with the verb is *to be,* as in the following examples.
e.g.   I *wasn't* at home.   We *weren't* at the party.
You *weren't* with her.
Marco *wasn't* so smart.   They *weren't* students.

Controlled Practice

Write each of the underlined past tense verbs in the negative form.

1.   My brother <u>met</u> his wife at a doctor's office.

_____

2.   Clara <u>enjoyed</u> reading murder mysteries.

_____

3.   That old man <u>was</u> my father.

_____

4   The deer <u>ran</u> across the road.

_____

5. The children <u>were</u> ready for their trip to Disney World.

_____

6. I <u>was</u> afraid of the dark.

_____

7. I <u>requested</u> a private room.

_____

8. The students <u>thought</u> the teacher was absent.

_____

9. We <u>wrote</u> her a thank you note.

_____

10. We <u>were</u> very bored during her class.

_____

Error Analysis

With a partner or in a small group, read the following stories and determine if the <u>underlined verbs</u> used the present and past tenses correctly. If the incorrect tense is used, revise it; however, if it is correct, do not change it.

1. Many years ago, my friend <u>starts</u> smoking in college, but after she <u>developed</u> chronic bronchitis and asthma, she <u>realizes</u> that her smoking <u>was caused</u> serious health problems, so she <u>quitted</u> smoking. Last week, my friend <u>when</u> to her doctor, because she <u>catched</u> a cold, and he <u>says</u> that she <u>needs</u> expensive medications to control her asthma.

2. About six years ago, when Elvin <u>is</u> 7 years old, his parents <u>enroll</u> him in a children's exercise program at the local gym because they <u>wanted</u> him to lose weight. After a few months, his parents <u>withdrawed</u> him from the program, because they <u>noticed</u> that he hadn't lost any weight and because he <u>not be</u> happy. Elvin <u>didn't participated</u> in the games or sports because he <u>is not</u> athletic and <u>didn't like</u> running around. In addition, he <u>though</u> the counselors at the program

36

were <u>not</u> sensitive to him. Worse yet, he <u>fell</u> depressed and <u>eated</u> more after he attended the program.

3.   In most hospitals, registered nurses usually <u>worked</u> at a desk, <u>manage</u> patient care and <u>distributing</u> medication. Most nurses <u>spent</u> their day communicating with their patients and other hospital staff members such as doctors. Registered nurses <u>didn't perform</u> a lot of heavy laborious duties. However, a nurse's aide is required to do manual labor such as lifting people and bathing each patient. Last night, I <u>given</u> fifteen sponge baths and <u>changed</u> the linen on thirty beds while the nurse <u>sits</u> in the nurses' station and <u>written</u> patient notes on the computer. Moreover, in most hospitals, even though nurses <u>worked</u> the same hours as the nurses' aides, the nurses <u>got</u> paid twice as much as the nurses' aides do. Last year, after the nurses <u>negotiate</u> a new contract, they <u>received</u> a large increase, while the aides <u>got</u> a small one that <u>is</u> lower than the inflation rate. As a consequence, I am attending college because I <u>wanted</u> to become a registered nurse and receive these benefits, too.

4.   When Katerina <u>arrive</u> in the United States, she <u>did not speaks</u> English well. She could hardly communicate with people because her language skills <u>was</u> limited. However, her parents <u>encouraging</u> her to go to college. It <u>took</u> her five years to complete her degree because English <u>is not</u> her first language. Today, Katerina has a good job and has become more self-confident and independent. In contrast, my cousin, Laura, <u>did not tried</u> to learn English when she <u>come</u> here ten years ago. Now, she <u>is depended</u> on other people to help her negotiate her business because she can't communicate effectively. Last year, when her neighbor <u>helped</u>

her do her banking, he <u>steals</u> money from her. If Laura had communicated well,

her neighbor could not have taken advantage of her. Clearly, immigrants who

<u>developed</u> good English skills <u>had</u> greater success in this country.

Forming Questions in the Past Tense

Read each of the following sentences and observe how the past tense is made negative.

I *ate* the candy.
Did you eat the candy?

You *studied* law.
Did you study law?

She *lost* her wallet.
Did she lose her wallet?

He *won* the prize.
Did he win the prize?

The dog barked for an hour.
Did the dog bark for an your?

My husband and I *went* to church yesterday.
Did you and your husband go to church?

The students *complained* about the difficult assignments.

Did the students complain about the difficult assignments?

A question is formed in the past tense by:

   a.   inserting the auxiliary verb *was/were* immediately after the subject and then by adding the *simple form of the verb*. e.g. *Marco was study* French in Paris?

   b.   inserting the word *did* before the subject of the sentence, and then the past participle of the verb. e.g. *Did Maria attended* the party?

   c.   inserting the auxiliary verb *did* immediately before the subject, and then inserting the *simple form of the verb*. e.g. *Did Alicia cry* at the wedding?

   d.   all of these

Answer [8]

---

[8] If you selected choice <u>c</u>, you are correct.

Read each of the following sentences, and observe how a past tense question is formed when the verb is *to be* (was or were).

Anoush *was* pregnant.
Was Anoush pregnant?

You *were* at the mall.
Were you at the mall?

She *was* very lazy.
Was she very lazy?

He *was* an artist.
Was he an artist?

The cat *was* hungry.
Was the cat hungry?

We *were* aware of the problem.
Were you aware of the problem?

Her parents *were* concerned about her safety.
Were her parents concerned about her safety?

When the verb *to be* is used in the past tense (was or were), a question is formed by:

a. inserting *did not* before the word *be*. e.g. *She did not be* absent?

b. inverting or switching the words *was* or *were* with the subject of the sentence.

   e.g. W*as she* sick?

c. inserting the word *not* before the words *to be*. e.g. *Carlos not be* absent?

Answer [9]

> **Forming Questions in the Past Tense**
>
> **Questions are formed in the past tense by inverting or switching the auxiliary verb did with the subject of the sentence.**
>
> e.g.   *Did you call* your mother?   *Did you eat* a plum?
>   *Did I purchase* the ticket?
>   *Did the bear* growl at him?   *Did they listen* to her?
>
> **However, when forming a past tense question with the verb *to be*, you must invert or switch the *subject* and the verb (*was* or *were*).**
>
> e.g.   *Were you* at home?   *Were you* upset?
>   *Was I* awake?
>   *Was the dog* friendly?   *Were those earrings* costly?

---

[9] If you selected <u>b</u>, you're correct.

39

Controlled Exercises

Use the rules just discussed to form questions from the following sentences.

1.   The babysitter took good care of my son.

   _____

2.   My husband caught the ball at the game.

   _____

3.   Paul and I were very tired.

   _____

4.   Elena was in her office early.

   _____

5.   I talked to Irina about the delay.

   _____

6.   The dog growled at the mailman.

   _____

7.   The music at the wedding was too loud.

   _____

8.   A car hit a deer by accident.

   _____

9.   Those students were absent several times.

   _____

10.   The doctor prescribed a new medication for my mother.

   _____

11.   You were kind to the old man.

   _____

12.   We wanted to buy a new car.

   _____

13.   It rained the entire week of our vacation.

   _____

14.   The thunder made a loud frightening sound.

   _____

15.   The information was inaccurate.

Practice Forming Questions in Context

Reread the article on page 23 of this chapter, and create five past tense questions that you would like to ask participants in the study or the researchers who conducted the investigation.

e.g. *Why did cognitive behavioral therapy reduce back pain the most?*

1. _____

2. _____

3. _____

4. _____

5. _____

Practice Writing

Select one of the following topics and write a composition. Be certain to use the past tense to describe events or actions that have already occurred, and the present tense to state facts and habits or routine behavior.

1. Write a composition describing a time you or a friend got hurt or injured. Describe how the injury occurred, how you felt and what you learned from this experience.

2. Write a composition explaining why younger people experience more pain than the older people.

The Progressive Tenses

The goal of this chapter is to instruct you in the form and use of the present and past progressive tenses.

Part One: The Present Progressive Tense

With a partner, read each sentence pair, and answer the questions that follow.

- a. I <u>wash</u> my hands regularly to remove dirt and germs.
- b I <u>am washing</u> my hands to remove the dirt and germs as I speak.

- a. You <u>listen</u> to music while you <u>study.</u>
- b. You <u>are listening</u> to music while you <u>are studying</u> for your history test.

- a. Stephen King <u>writes</u> mysteries.
- b. Stephen King <u>is writing</u> a new book right now.

- a. My husband and I <u>enjoy</u> watching old movies.
- b. My husband and I <u>are watching</u> an old movie entitled *Rear Window*.

- a. The children <u>like</u> to run under the sprinklers in the park.
- b. The children <u>are running</u> under the sprinklers at this moment.

In the five sentence pairs listed above, the tense of the <u>underlined</u> verb in letter <u>a</u> is:

- a. the present tense.

- b. the past tense.

- c. the present progressive tense.

- d. the past progressive tense.

Answer [1]

The present tense is used in letter <u>a</u> to:

- a. express two events that were occurring simultaneously (at the same time) in the past.

- b. express an event that already occurred.

- c. to express a fact or habitual behavior that occurs regularly.

- d. all of these.

Answer [2]

---

[1] If you selected choice <u>a</u>, you are correct.
[2] If you selected choice <u>c</u>, you are correct.

In the five sentence pairs, the tense of the <u>underlined</u> verb in letter <u>b</u> is:

    a. the present tense.

    b. the past tense.

    c. present perfect tense.

    d. the present progressive tense.

Answer [3]

The present progressive tense is used to express an activity that:

    a. is habitual or states a fact.

    b. is actively in progress.

    c. began in the past and continues in the present.

    d. was in progress in the past.

Answer [4]

To determine when to use the present progressive or the present tense, you should:

    a. determine if the action described is a habit or a fact, and then use the present tense. e.g. I *brush* my teeth three times a day.

    b. determine if the activity is occurring right now at the given moment and then use the present progressive tense. e.g. I *am brushing* my teeth right now.

    c. search for signal words that express habitual present tense behaviors such as every day, every year, regularly, routinely, in the morning. *Every evening my husband watches* the news.

    d. identify signal words that suggest an on-going present progressive action, such as right now, at the moment, at this time. *My husband is watching* the six o'clock news right now.

    e. all of these

Answer [5]

The Form of the Present Progressive Tense

Observe the form of the present progressive tense in the following examples.

---

[3] If you selected choice <u>d</u>, you are correct.
[4] If you selected choice <u>b</u>, you are correct.
[5] If you selected choice <u>e</u>, you are correct.

I <u>am speaking</u> to her now.   We <u>are eating</u> dinner at the moment.
I'<u>m speaking</u> to her now.   We'<u>re eating</u> dinner at the moment.

You <u>are exercising</u> right now.
You'<u>re exercising</u> right now.

She <u>is crying</u>.
He'<u>s crying</u>.   That house <u>is falling</u> apart.
             It'<u>s falling</u> apart.
The cake <u>is baking</u> in the oven.
It'<u>s baking</u> in the oven.

The present progressive tense is formed by:

a. inserting the subject of the sentence, the present tense of the verb to be (am, is or are), and the simple form of the verb. e.g. *Mary is listen* to music.
b. inserting the subject of the sentence, the present tense of the verb to be (am, is or are) and the present participle. e.g. *I am washing* my face.
c. inserting the subject and the present participle. e.g. *They washing*.
d. contracting the subject pronoun and the auxiliary verb (I'm, you're, he's, she's, it's, we're or they're) and adding the present participle. e.g. *We're watching* television.
e. b and d.

Answer [6]

What is a present participle? A present participle is:

a. the simple form of the verb plus the letters <u>ing</u>, such as walk<u>ing</u>.
b. the simple form of the verb plus the letters <u>ed</u>, such as walk<u>ed</u>.
c. an irregular verb.
d. none of these.

Answer [7]

Circle the list that contains present participles.

a. taken, given, been, seen.
b. taking, giving, being, seeing, walking.
c. is, am, are, to be
d. was and were.

Answer [8]

---

[6] If you selected choice <u>e</u>, you are correct.
[7] If you selected choice <u>a</u>, you are correct.
[8] If you selected choice <u>b</u>, you are correct.

What common mistake has the writer made in these sentences?

> Maria running to school.
> Amed and Sana talking on the phone.

The writer has:

a. used the past progressive tense.
b. used the wrong tense.
c. omitted (left out) the auxiliary verb <u>to be</u> (am, is, or are).
d. none of these.

Answer [9]

Form and Use of the Present Progressive Tense

Meaning

The present progressive tense expresses an activity that is *actively* in progress right now at the present moment.

e.g.   I *am writing* an essay.   We *are driving* to the mall.

        You *are learning* Arabic.

        He *is scolding* the child.
        She *is baking* a pie.   They *are cleaning* their bedrooms.
        The squirrel *is looking* for nuts.

The Form of Present Progressive Tense

The present progressive tense is formed by applying the following rule.

> Subject + present tense to be + present
>   (am, is or are)   participle

e.g.   I *am listening* to music.   We *are talking* during class.
        You *are writing* sentences.
        He *is lying* to his teacher.   They *are walking* home.

The subject pronouns (I, you, he, she, it, we and they) and the auxiliary verb (is, am or are) can be contracted in the present progressive.

e.g.   *I'm enjoying* the movie.   *We're taking* a walk.

        You're writing a note.

        It's raining heavily.   *They're cheering* for their team.

---

[9] If you selected choice <u>c</u>, you are correct.

Controlled Practice

Complete each of the following sentences with the either the present or the present progressive tense by observing signal words that suggest if an event is a fact, a habit or is occurring at the moment.

1. Every month after getting paid, Mary (buy) _____ a new dress or suit. Right now she (purchase) _____ a dress for a party.

2. We usually (celebrate) _____ my husband's birthday by eating at a nice restaurant. Because today is his birthday, we (dine) _____ in a fancy French restaurant in the City.

3. I usually (like) _____ to drink a cup of coffee, but I (drink) _____ hot chocolate right now.

4. My sister and her family (go) _____ to the movies every Saturday evening. Right now, they (watch) _____ a foreign film.

5. Eun Sun (like) _____ to eat Japanese food once a month. Right now she (eat) _____ sushi in a new restaurant in San Francisco.

6. After an opera performance, the audience usually (clap) _____ their hands. While the audience (clap) _____, the performers bow to express thanks for the applause.

7. Please quiet down. The children (do) _____their homework. They (do) _____ their homework every evening after dinner.

8. Although I (hate) _____ to talk on the phone, I (speak) _____ to my cousin at this moment because I want to know if my uncle is all right.

9. It is a lousy day. The snow (fall) _____ heavily, and the wind (blow) _____ at thirty miles per hour.

10. I (call) _____ my husband at work every afternoon. I (dial) _____ his cell phone number as we speak.

Practice Writing Sentences in the Present Progressive Tense

Take a walk around the college campus and select one location that interests you. Write a paragraph describing what is occurring in this area.

e.g. *Right now, I am sitting outside the cafeteria. I am observing all the activities that are occurring there. One woman is reading a book while she is drinking bottled water. A couple of young men are sitting at a table and talking to each other. One of them is pointing to a guy who is waiting on line to pay for his food. The men and women behind the counter are cooking the food, and they are also cleaning the grill.*

The Negative Form of the Present Progressive Tense

Observe how the present progressive tense is made negative.

I *am not lying.*   We *are not listening.*

You *are not studying.*

He *is not yelling.*
She *is not living* in Korea.   They *are not reading.*
That lion *is not pacing* in his cage.

The present progressive tense is made negative by inserting the subject:

a. the auxiliary verb *do/does*, the word *not*, and the present participle. e.g. She *does not studying.*

b. the word *am, is,* or *are* , the word *not*, and the *present participle.* e.g. I <u>*am not cleaning*</u> my house at this time.

c. the word *not* before the words *to be.* e.g. We <u>*not be writing*</u> a composition.

d. none of these.

Answer [10]

---
[10] If you selected choice <u>b</u>, you are correct.

The Negative Form of the Present Progressive Tense

The **present progressive** tense is made negative by using the following rule.

> Subject + present tense to be + not + present
> am, is or are   participle

e.g.   *I am not talking.*   We *are not cheating.*

You *are not listening.*

She *is not learning* anything.
He *is not eating.*   They *are not playing* cards.
The cat *is not drinking* the milk.

Note: contractions can also be used in the present progressive tense.

e.g.   *I'm not lying* to you.   We *'re not working* late.

You *aren't dreaming.*

She *isn't sleeping.*
He *isn't driving* the car.   They *aren't listening* to me.
They *aren't singing.*

Controlled Practice

Make each of the underlined verbs negative in the present progressive test.

1. Whenever I look in Yelena's bedroom, she <u>is sending</u> instant messages to her friends.

   _____

2. Each morning, when I walk into the kitchen, my father <u>is reading</u> the paper.

   _____

3. My sister-in-law <u>is undergoing</u> surgery now.

   _____

4. When the professor notices that students <u>are listening</u> during class, she gets annoyed.

   _____

5. I <u>am working</u> late today.

   _____

6. We're eating french fries.

   _____

7. You are trying to stop smoking.

   _____

8. The dog is begging for food at the table.

   _____

9. My parents are traveling to Europe with me.

   _____

10. Vincenzo and I are swimming in a competition .

   _____

Practice in Context

Read the following article and determine when and where to use the simple present or present progressive tenses.

Years ago, first impressions were often made in person; however, the Internet has changed the way that people become acquainted, so that many initial meetings (occur) _____ in cyberspace, not face-to-face. Consequently, people (begin) _____ to plan how to present themselves on-line so that their image (appeal) _____ to multiple audiences, such as friends, relatives, co-workers, and potential employers.

As a result of social networking sites, psychologists (examine now) _____ the online world through the concept of impression management because they (believe) _____ many people are unsure about how to present themselves. While some people (gear) _____ their image toward a

49

specific audience, others (display) _____ their best image inasmuch as

potential employers may not be inclined to hire a recent college graduate who (play

always) _____ beer pong in his/her Facebook pictures.

In general, psychologists (believe not) _____ impression management

(be) _____deceptive, but a way to seize the attention of others. In fact, these

studies have indicated that when people (misrepresent) _____ themselves, it

is often because they (try) _____ to communicate an idealized portrait of

themselves. Moreover, even when some people (shave) _____ a few years

off their real age on dating websites, most people (contend) _____ this

is acceptable and a harmless white lie.

Nonetheless, despite warnings, some users (continue) _____ to

post outrageous photographs of themselves while they (drink) _____ heavily or

(use) _____ drugs. However, what they don't realize is that they (reveal)

_____ deeply personal information within these images that may remain in

cyberspace forever. This conduct (suggest also) _____ that they (lack)

_____ discretion, or they (believe) _____ their future

cannot be compromised by such pictures. Some researchers have proposed that such

users (enjoy) _____ the risk of posting these images, and may even derive

pleasure from them.

Clearly, when people of all ages (post) _____ pictures and

information about themselves on-line, they must be cognizant of the image they project

for their diverse cyber-space audiences.

Error Analysis

Read the following paragraph and determine if the writer has used the <u>underlined</u> present and present progressive tense verbs correctly. If there is a mistake, correct it. But, *do not* correct a verb that is not underlined.

Anger and moodiness <u>are</u> powerful emotions that can interfere with a person's performance at a job. Many employers <u>are expecting</u> their employees to be pleasant when they <u>are interacting</u> with customers. Most businesses <u>want</u> their employees to greet customers with a welcoming smile. However, many people <u>arrive</u> at work angry and in a terrible mood. This foul mood usually <u>affecting</u> their attitude at work, because an irritable secretary, salesperson or waiter <u>is turning</u> off valued customers. Right now, I <u>sitting</u> in a coffee shop. Even though an older man <u>waits</u> for service, a young female employee <u>holds</u> a loud, angry cell phone conversation with her boyfriend. While she <u>is arguing</u> with her boyfriend, she has turned her back to the three customers who <u>are waiting</u> on line.

Finally, after one customer <u>demands</u> service, the young woman <u>is strolling</u> over to the counter. But, she utters a nasty remark so that the man <u>is knowing</u> that she doesn't want to serve him. As she approaches the man, another customer says, "She <u>thinks</u> we're here to service her." This incident <u>suggests</u> that being in a foul mood <u>is affecting</u> an employee's performance and attitude.

Practice Writing

Take three pictures from a magazine, newspaper or book. For each picture, write a paragraph describing what is happening in the picture.

Part Two: The Past Progressive Tense

In the second half of this chapter, you will learn how to use and form the past progressive tense, which is very similar to the present progressive, except that it refers to an action that was actively in progress in the past.

The Meaning of the Past Progressive Tense

With a partner or in a small group, read each sentence pair and specify the tense used by the underlined verb.

   a. When I <u>was walking</u> in the door, the phone rang.

   b. As Chris raced through the finish line, everyone <u>was cheering.</u>

   c. While the women <u>were chatting</u>, the children <u>were playing</u> in the park.

   d. While we <u>were singing and dancing,</u> the mailman <u>was banging</u> on the door.

In these sentences, the tense of the <u>underlined</u> verbs is:

   a. the present tense.

   b. the past tense.

   c. the present progressive tense.

   d. the past progressive tense.

Answer [11]

The past progressive tense expresses:

   a. events that were in progress or occurring in the past.

   b. an event that already occurred.

   c. a fact or habitual behavior that occurred regularly in the past.

   d. all of these.

Answer [12]

Read the following sentence and respond to the question below it.

   While we <u>were singing and dancing,</u> the mailman <u>was banging</u> on the door.

The past progressive tense is used twice in this sentence to describe two:

   a. events that were in progress at the same time in the past.

   b. events that already occurred.

   c. habitual activities that occurred regularly in the past.

   d. all of these.

Answer [13]

---

[11] If you selected choice <u>d</u>, you are correct.
[12] If you selected choice <u>a</u>, you are correct.

Read the following sentence, and respond to the question below it.

past   past
↓ tense   ↓ progressive

As Chris <u>raced</u> through the finish line, everyone <u>was cheering</u>.

The simple past and the past progressive tenses are both used in this sentence to:

    a. describe two habitual activities that occurred regularly in the past.

    b. two events that began in the past and continue in the present.

    c. describe one event that was in progress while another event finished.

    d. all of these.

Answer [14]

The Form of the Past Progressive Tense

Examine how the past progressive tense is formed in the following examples.

I <u>was discussing</u> the death penalty.   We <u>were debating</u> arranged marriages.

You <u>were talking</u> on a cell phone
while you <u>were driving</u> the car.

The child <u>was laughing</u> at the clown.
The man <u>was waiting</u> for his wife.   My parents <u>were decorating</u> their house.
The tiger <u>was running</u> quickly.

The past progressive tense is formed by inserting the subject plus:

    a. the past tense of the verb *to be.* (was or were) e.g. They *were.*

    b. the past tense of the auxiliary verb to be (was or were), and the past participle (walked, talked, listened, etc.). e.g. We *were talked* loudly.

    c. the past tense of the auxiliary verb to be (was or were) and the present participle (walking, talking, singing, etc). I *was walking* home.

    d. none of these.

Answer [15]

The difference in meaning between the simple past tense and the past progressive tense is:

    a. the past tense expresses an action that is completed and already finished.

---

[13] If you selected choice <u>a</u>, you are correct.

[14] If you selected choice <u>c</u>, you are correct.

[15] If you selected choice <u>c</u>, you are correct.

b. the past progressive tense emphasizes an action(s) that was/were in progress in the past.

c. the past progressive tense describes an action that began in the past and continues into the future.

d. a and b

Answer [16]

Therefore, the past progressive can be used along with the:

a. simple past tense.

b. simple present tense and no other tense.

c. present progressive and the present perfect tenses.

d. none of these

Answer [17]

Form and Meaning of the Past Progressive Tense

Meaning

The past progressive tense expresses an activity that was *actively* in progress at a time in the past. It emphasizes the *duration* or *continuation* of an event in progress.

e.g.   I *was learning* French, while they *were studying* physics.
        You *were writing* a letter, when my mother arrived.
        He *was making* spaghetti, while she *was drinking* coffee.
        She *was cleaning* the house, while the children *were playing*.

Form of Past Progressive Tense

The past progressive tense is formed as follows.

Subject +   past tense to be   +   present
            (was were)   participle

e.g.   I *was walking* the dog.   We *were arguing* during that time.

        You *were drafting* a paper.

        He *was cooking* when I called.   They *were wasting* time playing on
                                           the computer.

---

[16] If you selected choice <u>d</u>, you are correct.
[17] If you selected choice <u>a</u>, you are correct.

Controlled Practice

Complete each of the following sentences with the either the <u>past</u> or the <u>past progressive</u> tense by observing signal words that specify if an event was completed or occurring in the past.

1. Mario and Louisa (eat) _____ a big steak dinner when Sofia walked in

    the door.

2. While I (prepare) _____ a meal, my husband (watch) _____

    the football game.

3. When the professor (walk) _____ in the classroom, the student (discuss)

    _____ the homework assignment.

4. Early this morning I (go) _____ to the library to study for an exam. While I

    (review) _____ my notes, a woman (tap) _____ me on the

    shoulder. When I (look) _____ up, I was surprised to see it was my cousin, Ali.

    He (sit) _____ down next to me, and we (start) _____ to talk. While we

    (chat) _____, several people (give) _____ us dirty looks because we

    (disturb) _____ them. So, we (leave) _____ the library

    and (go) _____ to the cafeteria.

5. Yesterday, my company (interview) _____ five people for an accountant's

    job. While my boss (converse) _____ with one woman, her cell phone (ring)

    _____, and she (answer) _____ it. While she (talk) _____ to

    her friend, the manager (tap) _____ his fingers impatiently so that the

    woman would know he was annoyed. Finally, when my boss (ask) _____ her

    to hang up, the woman (become) _____ offended and (storm) _____ out

55

of the office. Another young man (text) _____ his friend while he (talk) _____ to the interviewer.

Practice Writing

With a partner, make a list of three activities you, or a classmate were doing while the professor was teaching the class.

e.g. *While I was looking out the window, the teacher was explaining the past progressive tense to the class. However, one student, Mario, was listening carefully because he wanted to understand how to use this tense.*

Practice in Context

Read the following story, and insert the simple past or past progressive tenses in the blanks provided.

While a teenager in upstate New York (drive) _____ an SUV and (send) _____ text messages, she (crash) _____ into a huge tractor-trailer. This incident and others has highlighted the need for a law to prohibit drivers from sending text messages when they're behind the wheel of a car.

By examining the driver's cell phone records, the police (determine) _____ that the teenage driver (send) _____ and (receive) _____ text messages when her SUV (run) _____ into the back of the tractor-trailer. This accident (kill) _____ the driver and her four girls who had just graduated from high school. Tests (perform) _____ on the driver after the deadly crash (demonstrate) _____ that the primary cause of the accident (be) _____ driver inattention due to the apparent text messaging. No alcohol or drugs were involved.

Worse yet, a recent poll of people 18 to 24 years old (reveal) _____ that two out of three confess to sending text messages when they drive. In view of this incident, under a newly proposed law, anyone (catch) _____ texting while they (drive) _____ could be fined up to $100, which is the same penalty that applies now when police catch drivers conversing on cell phones.

The Negative Form of the Past Progressive Tense

The following are examples of the past progressive tense in the negative form.

I *was not talking* at that moment.   We *were not losing* the game

You *were not studying*.

He *was not walking*.
She *was not complaining*.   They *were not driving*.
That woman *was not playing* a guitar.

The past progressive tense is made negative by inserting the subject:

a.   the word *not*, the words *to be* and the *present participle*. e.g. We <u>not be writing</u> a composition.

b.   the auxiliary verb *did*, the word *not* and the *present participle*. e.g. She *did not singing* the national anthem.

c.   the auxiliary verb *was* or *were*, the word *not*, and the *present participle*. e.g. I <u>was not taking</u> a nap.

d.   none of these.

Answer [18]

------

[18] If you selected choice <u>c</u>, you are correct.

The Negative Form of the Past Progressive Tenses

The past progressive tense is made negative by applying the following rule.

      Subject + past tense + not + present
                to be   participle

  e.g.   I *was not singing*.   We *were not eating* candy.

          You *were not watching* her.

          He *was not drinking* soda.
          She *was not eating* cake.   They *were not screaming*.
          The car *was not starting*.

Note: contractions can also be used in the past progressive tense.

  e.g.   I *wasn't dating* her.   We *weren't enjoying* the food.

          You *weren't sleeping*.

          She *wasn't watching* him.   They *weren't talking* to us.

Controlled Practice

Convert each of the <u>underlined</u> verbs to the negative form of the past progressive tense.

1. My brother <u>was watching</u> an action movie when I walked in the door.

    _____

2. When the waiter arrived, we <u>were looking</u> at the menu.

    _____

3. The lawyer <u>was preparing</u> his case until late in the evening.

    _____

4. My aunt <u>was relocating</u> to Chicago.

    _____

5. Mariana <u>was living</u> in a big house in Brazil.

    _____

6. Her family <u>was living</u> in a big fancy house.

_____

7. You <u>were attending</u> every single class.

_____

8. We <u>were planning</u> a big party for them.

_____

9. The truck <u>was using</u> a lot of gas.

_____

10. The police officers <u>were stopping</u> cars on the highway.

_____

Practice Writing

With a partner, make a list of three activities you, your friends, family or teachers *were not doing* before you entered college.

e.g. *Before I entered college, I wasn't learning much English because I wasn't interacting with anyone who spoke English. Instead, I was working in a place where everyone spoke Cantonese. Therefore, my co-workers and I weren't getting the opportunity to practice our English. Consequently, we were not improving our English at all.*

Forming Questions in the Present and Past Progressive Tenses

Observe the following examples to determine how a question is formed in the present progressive tense.

I am lying.
Am I lying?

We are watching television.
Are we watching television?

You are typing.
Are you typing?

He is eating dinner.
Is he eating dinner?

She is shopping.
Is she shopping?

They are playing cards.
Are they playing cards?

Questions are formed in the present progressive tense by:

    a. inverting (switching) the auxiliary verbs *am, is, are* and the subject.
        e.g. *Were you* dating Paolo?

    b. inserting *does* or *do* before the subject and then by adding the present participle
        e.g. *Does Pamela watching* the movie?

    c. deleting the subject, then switching the auxiliary verb, *am, is, are* with the present participle. e.g. *Are listening* to the radio?

    d. a and b.

Answer [19]

Observe the following examples that describe how a question is formed in the past progressive tense.

I was teasing him.
Was I teasing him?

We were talking.
Were we talking?

You were writing your paper.
Were you writing your paper?

He was baking a cake.
Was he baking a cake?

She was sewing.
Was she sewing?

They were playing cards.
Were they playing cards?

Questions are formed in the past progressive tenses by:

    a. inserting *did* before the subject, and then by adding the present participle. e.g. *Did Usman looking* for a job?

    b. inverting (switching) the auxiliary verbs *was* or *were* and the subject. e.g. *Were you* dating Paolo?

    c. deleting the subject, then switching the auxiliary verb *was* and *were* with the present participle. e.g. *Was writing* a letter to her mother?

    d. a and b.

Answer [20]

---

[19] If you selected choice <u>a</u>, you are correct.
[20] If you selected choice <u>b</u>, you are correct.

Forming Questions in the Present Progressive and Past Progressive

Present Progressive Questions

A question is formed in the present progressive tense by switching the subject and the auxiliary verb (am, is or are).

e.g.
Am I listening to you?   *Are we leaving* now?

Are you eating?

Is she taking a shower?
Is he taking a bath?   *Are they playing* a game?
Is the cat drinking milk?

Past Progressive Questions

A question is formed in the past progressive tense by switching the subject and the auxiliary verb (was or were).

e.g.
Was I reading a book?   *Were we telling* the truth?

Were you watching her?

Was he buying a car?
Was she eating candy?   *Were the children screaming?*
Was the house getting warm?

Controlled Practice

Convert each of the following sentences into questions, but be certain to observe if the verb is in the present progressive or the past progressive.

1. My daughter <u>was dialing</u> the phone.

   _____

2. We <u>were waiting</u> on line for fifteen minutes.

   _____

3. My sister <u>is always complaining</u>.

   _____

4. The students <u>were hoping</u> the class would be easy.

   _____

5. I <u>was looking</u> out my bedroom window when the robbery occurred.

   _____

6. My students <u>were writing</u> an essay.

   _____

7. They <u>are always claiming</u> they don't have enough money.

   _____

8. I <u>am baking</u> a cream cheese pound cake for the party.

   _____

9. I <u>was sleeping</u> when the door bell rang.

   _____

10. Elena <u>was worrying</u> about her health when she started college.

   _____

Practice Writing

Pretend you witnessed a robbery and you now have to prepare a statement of the events for the police. Write a paragraph using the simple past and past progressive tenses to describe the crime.

e.g. *While I <u>was cleaning</u> the windows in my apartment, I <u>saw</u> a young man jump out of a van. As he <u>was running</u> down the street, he <u>grabbed</u> an older woman's purse. While the lady <u>was yelling</u> "Help! Help!" an off duty police officer <u>jumped</u> out of his car and <u>began</u> to chase the robber. As the robber <u>was dashing</u> down the street, he <u>tripped</u> and <u>fell</u> so that the police officer <u>caught</u> and <u>apprehended</u> him.*

Error Analysis

Read the following paragraphs and determine if the writer has used the underlined past and past progressive tense verbs correctly. If there is a mistake, correct it. But, *do not* correct a verb that is not underlined.

While my friend, Alejandro, <u>driving</u> on the freeway, he <u>was trying</u> to look at his Global Positioning Unit (GPS) because he <u>realized</u> that he was lost. While he <u>was using</u> his GPS, he <u>was taking</u> his eyes off the road, and his car accidentally <u>began</u> to swerve into another lane. As Alejandro's car <u>veered</u> into the left land, a big truck <u>was racing</u> down the left lane. The truck driver <u>was honking</u> his horn to alert Alejandro, but Alejandro <u>became</u> so nervous that he <u>was hitting</u> the gas pedal instead of the break. Even though the truck driver <u>was trying</u> to avoid Alejandro's vehicle, he <u>struck</u> Alejandro's car and another one.

Immediately after the accident, all three vehicles <u>pulled</u> off the highway to exchange information. As soon as Alejandro <u>exited</u> his car, the two other drivers <u>were yelling</u> at him because he <u>read</u> a map while he <u>driving</u> a car. Fortunately, a police officer <u>arrived</u> and <u>was calming</u> everyone down.

A few months after the accident, Alejandro's insurance company <u>was raising</u> his car insurance rate because they <u>believed</u> his behavior <u>was</u> reckless and irresponsible. After this expensive incident, Alejandro <u>learned</u> that when he is driving a car, he can not be distracted by other activities.

The Present Perfect Tense

The goal of this chapter is to teach you:

- the difference between the present perfect and the past tenses;
- the form of the present perfect tense;
- the use of regular and irregular past participles in the present perfect tense

The Meaning of the Present Perfect Tense

The present perfect tense is used to express events that:

1. were completed at an indefinite or uncertain time in the past;

2. began in the past, but continue in the present; and

3. were repeated an indefinite or unknown number of times in the past.

The next three sections will explain this detail.

The First Use of the Present Perfect Tense

With a partner or in a small group, read each sentence pair and answer the questions that follow.

   a. I <u>have seen</u> this movie before.
   b I <u>saw</u> this movie last year.

   a. You <u>have discussed</u> this issue previously.
   b. You <u>discussed</u> this issue last week.

   a. Raj <u>has traveled</u> to India.
   b. Raj <u>traveled</u> to India three years ago.

   a. We <u>have toured</u> South America.
   b. We <u>toured</u> to South America two years ago.

   a. They <u>have eaten</u> at that restaurant.
   b. They <u>ate</u> at that restaurant on Sunday evening.

What tense is used in letter <u>a</u> of each sentence pair?

   a. the simple present tense

   b. the past perfect tense

   c. the simple past tense

d. the present perfect tense

Answer [1]

What tense is used in letter b of each sentence pair?

    a. the simple present tense

    b. the past perfect tense

    c. the simple past tense

    d. the present perfect tense

Answer [2]

The past tense is used in these sentences because it describes an action that:

    a. was completed at a definite time in the past.

    b. was completed at an indefinite time in the past.

    c. was continuous in the past.

    d. all of these

Answer [3]

The present perfect tense is used because it describes an action that:

    a. was completed at a definite time in the past.

    b. was completed at an indefinite time in the past.

    c. is continuous.

    d. all of these

Answer [4]

The Second Use of the Present Perfect Tense

In a small group, read each set of sentence pairs and answer the questions that follow.

    a. We <u>have lived</u> in Texas since 2003.
    b   We <u>lived</u> in Texas for five years.

    a. You <u>have criticized</u> Mateo since you first met him.
    b. You <u>criticized</u> Mateo for almost two years.

---

[1] If you selected choice d, you are correct.
[2] If you selected choice c, you are correct.
[3] If you selected choice a, you are correct.
[4] If you selected choice b, you are correct.

a. Julio <u>has been</u> sick for two weeks.

b. Julio <u>was</u> sick for two weeks.

What tense is used in letter <u>a</u> of each sentence pair?

a. the present perfect tense

b. the simple present tense

c. the past perfect tense

d. the simple past tense

Answer [5]

What tense is used in letter <u>b</u> of each sentence pair?

a. the present progressive

b. the past perfect

c. the present perfect

d. the simple past

Answer [6]

In these examples, the *past tense* is used because it describes an action that:

a. is completed and finished.

b. began in the past and continues in the present.

c. never occurred.

d. was continuous in past time.

Answer [7]

In these examples, the *present perfect tense* is used because it describes an action that:

a. was completed at an unknown past time.

b. was completed at a known past time.

c. began in the past and continues in the present.

d. all of these

Answer [8]

---

[5] If you selected choice <u>a</u>, you are correct.
[6] If you selected choice <u>d</u>, you are correct.
[7] If you selected choice <u>a</u>, you are correct.
[8] If you selected choice <u>c</u>, you are correct.

The signal word(s) that indicate that these actions begin in the past, but continue in the present are:

   a. for

   b. since

   c. had

   d. a and b

Answer [9]

The Third Use of the Present Perfect Tense

With a partner or in a small group, read each pair of sentences and answer the questions below.

   a. We <u>have requested</u> assistance on several occasions.
   b We <u>requested</u> assistance five times.

   a. Those students <u>have been</u> late countless times.
   b. Those students <u>were</u> late twelve times.

   a. Antonia <u>has visited</u> her parents numerous times.
   b. Antonia <u>visited</u> her parents three times.

What tense is used in letter <u>a</u> of each pair of sentences?

   a. the simple past

   b. the simple present

   c. the present perfect tense

   d. the past perfect tense

Answer [10]

What tense is used in letter <u>b</u> of each pair of sentences?

   a. the past progressive

   b. the simple past

   c. the present perfect

   d. the simple present

Answer [11]

In these examples, the past tense is used because it describes an action that:

---

[9] If you selected choice <u>d</u>, you are correct.
[10] If you selected choice <u>c</u>, you are correct.
[11] If you selected choice <u>b</u>, you are correct.

a. occurred an indefinite number of times in the past.

b. began in the past and continues in the present.

c. occurred a definite number of times in the past.

d. was progressive in present time.

Answer [12]

In these examples, the present perfect tense is used because it describes an action that:

a. was completed at a definite time in the past.

b. was occurring in the present.

c. began in the past and continues in the future.

d. occurred an indefinite number of times in the past.

Answer [13]

The Three Meaning of the Present Perfect Tense

The present perfect tense is used to express an action that:

1. was completed at an indefinite time in the past.

   e.g.   I *have seen* those teenagers before.
          She *has taken* this bus with me previously.

2. began in the past and continues in the present.

   e.g.   We *have attended* this college since 2007.
          You *have been* on the phone for more than two hours.

3. occurred an indefinite number of times in the past.

   e.g.   They *have interrupted* this class with their noise on numerous occasions.
          My husband and I *have traveled* to China many times.

---

[12] If you selected choice <u>c</u>, you are correct.

[13] If you selected choice <u>d</u>, you are correct.

Forming the Present Perfect Tense

I <u>have written</u> many letters to him.

You <u>have been</u> absent on numerous occasions.

That woman <u>has been</u> ill for days.
The man <u>has lied</u> before.
That dog <u>has barked</u> for hours.

We <u>have studied</u> for hours.

They <u>have taken</u> advantage of their parents in the past.

The present perfect tense is formed by inserting:

a. the subject of the sentence, and the past participle of the verb. e.g. *She taken* the test.

b. the subject of the sentence, the past tense of the verb have (had) and the present participle. e.g. *She had taking* the test.

c. the subject of the sentence, the present tense of the verb have (has or have) and the past participle. e.g. *She has taken* the test.

d. the subject and the present participle. e.g. *She taking* the test

Answer [14]

What is a past participle? A past participle is:

a. the simple form of the verb plus the letters <u>ing,</u> such as *walk<u>ing</u>* and *read<u>ing</u>*.

b. the simple form of the verb plus the letters <u>ed</u> or <u>d</u> such as in *walk<u>ed</u>* or *believ<u>ed</u>*.

c. an irregular verb such as *went, did, began.*

d. none of these.

Answer [15]

Circle the list that contains past participles.

a. talked, played, wanted, experienced.

b. taking, giving, being, seeing, walking.

c. is, am, are, was, were, had

d. to walk, to study, to think

Answer [16]

---

[14] If you selected choice <u>c</u>, you are correct.
[15] If you selected choice <u>b</u>, you are correct.
[16] If you selected choice <u>a</u>, you are correct.

How is the past participle formed when a verb ends in the letter *y*?

    a. When the verb ends in the letter *y*, just add the letters *ed* such as *annoyed* or *studyed*.

    b. If the *y* is preceded by a vowel, add the letters *ed*, unless it is an irregular verb such as *employed*.

    c. If the *y* is preceded by a consonant, change the letter *y* to the letter *i* and add the letters *ed* such as *carried*.

    d. choice b and c.

Answer [17]

Observe the following examples.

e.g.   (worry) Many children have occup*ied* themselves on the Internet for years.

        (annoy) My company has employ*ed* him since 2008.

The Past Participle of Irregular Verbs

In English, many verbs have irregular past participles. A complete list of the most common past participles is provided in **Appendix A**. However, you must be careful not to confuse the irregular past tense verbs with the irregular past participles as in the following examples.

Read these sentences and determine what has been done incorrectly.

    Anna has *went* to that restaurant many times.

    I have *drank* wine before.

    She has *came* home late frequently.

In these sentences, the writer used:

    a. the simple past tense, instead of the present perfect tense.

    b. the irregular past tense verb, instead of the irregular past participle.

    c. the past perfect tense, instead of the simple past tense.

    d. none of these.

Answer [18]

---

[17] If you selected choice <u>d</u>, you are correct.

[18] If you chose letter <u>b</u>, you are correct.

In present perfect tense, you can also insert an adverb between the auxiliary verbs (has or have) and the past participle. Observe the following examples.

I *haven't always been* so patient.   We *have never lied* to her.

You *have hardly eaten* a thing.

He *has barely known* her two weeks.
She *has frequently yelled* at me.   They *have just mailed* the check.
It *has never rained* for three weeks.

Forming Present Perfect Tense

The present perfect tense uses the following format:

> Subject + present tense have + past
> has or have   participle

e.g.   I *have drunk* soda for years.   We *have had* a pet before.
        You *have wasted* my time before.
        Maria *has always complained*.   They *have helped* at times.

You can also use contractions with the present perfect tense as demonstrated in the following examples.

e.g.   *I've loved* him for years.   *We've had* problems before.
        You've spent carelessly.
        She's always disliked him.   *They've told* us many times.

An adverb can also be inserted between the auxiliary verb (has or have) and the past participle such as in the following examples.

e.g.   I have *always* been available.   We have *just* arrived.
        You have *already* lied once.
        He has *rarely* complained.   They have *barely* spoken.

In English, many of the past participles are irregular; therefore, it is necessary to check Appendix A to verify the correct spelling.

Controlled Practice

Read each of the following sentences and determine if you should use the simple past or the present perfect tense. Be certain to look for clues that specify which tense should be used and consult Appendix A to verify the correct form of irregular past participles and past tense verbs.

1. Alejandro (go) _____ to work early today. For the past few weeks, he (go) _____ into the office early because his company is installing a new computer system.

2. Throughout the years, that talk show host (give) _____ some terrible advise to some of his guests. Last week he (tell) _____ a woman to hit her three year old son when he was naughty.

3. She is a famous artist. She (draw) _____ many pictures that are displayed at the Museum of Modern Art.

4. Yesterday, when Mr. Cocero's dog escaped from the yard, it (chase) _____ two small children. Over the years, that dog (chase) _____ countless numbers of people as they (walk) _____ down this block.

5. I (know) _____ Karina since I was five years old. We (meet) _____ in first grade.

6. The sun (rise) _____ at 6:54 this morning, and it (rise) _____ in the east since the beginning of time.

7. At the game on Sunday, Pasquale (throw) _____ the ball across the field. He (throw) _____ the ball out of the park on many occasions.

8. Larissa (swim) _____ in two races last night. She (swim) _____ in numerous competitions at her college.

9. Stephen (want) _____ to learn to drive a motorcycle for ages, so he (take) _____ two lessons last week.

10. Cristafano (write) _____ many books over the years. He (have) _____ a best seller last year.

Practice in Context

Read the following article, and use the rules just learned to determine if you should complete the blanks with the simple past or the present perfect tenses.

For years, dogs (play) _____ a special role in the world of medicine. Since they have been trained to guide blind people and to hear for the deaf, dogs (become) _____ indispensible to disabled people.

Some recent studies (demonstrate also) _____ dogs have an even greater impact on humans. One investigator (discover) _____ pet owners made fewer visits to the doctor. An Australian researcher (illustrate) _____ that dog owners (have) _____ lower cholesterol, blood pressure and fewer heart problems in contrast to people who do not own pets.

Some dogs (warn, even) _____ their owners of looming health threats. In fact, researchers (notice) _____ over the years that some dogs (have) _____ the instinctive ability to sense when their owners were about to have a epileptic seizure.

Practice Writing

1. Write a paragraph describing an activity that you began in the past and continue to perform in the present.

e.g. *I have worked at that store since 2008. I started working there immediately after I graduated from high school. I worked in the children's department for six months. However, I have worked in the shoe department since I received a promotion last month.*

_____

_____

_____

_____

2. Write a paragraph describing an activity that you performed at an indefinite time in the past.

e.g. *I have gone to that movie theatre many times, but I don't remember when I went there last. In fact, I have seen The Bourne Identity at that theatre countless times.*

_____

_____

_____

_____

3. Write a paragraph describing an activity that you performed many times in the past.

e.g. *In all the years I have gone to school, I have done countless homework assignments. In recent years, I have completed most of my homework on a computer, but one time when my computer crashed, I used a typewriter. Since that time, I have not had to work on a typewriter.*

_____

_____

_____

_____

Negation: Making the Present Perfect Tense Negative

Read each of the following sentences and observe how the present perfect tense is made negative.

I *have not eaten* dinner yet.

You *have not listened* to me.

She *has not seen* him for years.

He *has not been* aware of the problem.

That woman *has not confirmed* the appointment.

We *have not taken* physics before.

The teachers *have not marked* the final exams yet.

The present perfect tense is made negative by:

a. inserting the auxiliary verb *had* immediately after the subject, the word *not*, and the *simple form of the verb.* e.g. She *had not eat* yet.

b. inserting the word *not* immediately after the auxiliary verb *have or has*, but before the *past participle* of the verb. e.g. She *has not eaten* yet.

c. inserting the auxiliary verb *have or has,* the word *not* and *past tense* of the verb. e.g. She *has not ate* yet.

d. all of these

Answer [19]

When the present perfect tense is negative, you can also use contractions as in the following examples.

I *haven't learned* much English yet.   We *haven't baked* many pies.

You *haven't informed* her.

He *hasn't known* her too long.
She *hasn't asked* many questions   They *haven't obeyed* any of the rules.
It *hasn't rained* for weeks.

The Negative Form of the Present Perfect Tense

The present perfect tense is made negative by using the following rule:

Subject + present tense of have + not + past
        (has or have)   participle

e.g.   I *have not drunk* any wine.   We *have not had* to wait long.
      You *have not spent* much money.
      Maria *has not spoken* to him.   They *have not taken* care of her.

You can also use contractions in the present perfect tense, as in the following examples.

e.g.   I *haven't yelled* at her.   We *haven't had* enough time.
      You *haven't heard* from her.
      Maria *hasn't criticized* at him.   They *haven't* lost any money.

Controlled Practice

Insert the negative form of the present perfect tense in the following statements.

1. When will Carlos ever marry Marta?

---

[19] If you selected choice <u>b</u>, you are correct.

Carlos (not, propose) _____ to Marta yet because he is afraid that she

will refuse to marry him.

2. Why don't you go to Peru this summer?

    I have traveled to Peru countless times, but I (go, not) _____ to

    Argentina ever before.

3. Since Bao (not, visit) _____ his parents in years, he will travel to

    Vietnam this summer.

4. Farida (not, return) _____ college since she gave birth to her

    son.

5. My husband and I (not live) _____ in San Francisco since last year.

6. The professor (not, meet) _____ with Enrique yet.

7. Alicia (not, work) _____ at a department store since she graduated

    from high school.

8. It's obvious that you (not, have) _____ the opportunity to work with

    a computer before.

9. They (not, eat) _____ fast food for dinner many times.

10. When will you pay your tuition?

    I (not, pay) _____ my tuition because I don't have enough money.

Error Analysis

Read each of the following short paragraphs and determine if the underlined words use the present perfect and past tenses correctly. If an incorrect tense is used, revise it according to the rules learned in this chapter.

1. For the past thirty years, computer technology <u>has develops</u> very rapidly, but many

    workers <u>didn't develop</u> computer skills so that they <u>became</u> less marketable in today's

    economy. My aunt <u>was</u> a legal secretary before she <u>had</u> children. Recently, when she tried to get a job, she was rejected by many companies because she <u>didn't learn</u> to word process a document or use e-mail yet.

2. My friend, Amir, <u>smoked</u> since high school. He wants to quit, but he is addicted and can't kick the habit by himself. He would participate in a smoke enders program, but because these programs are so expensive, my friend can't afford one. As a result, he <u>didn't give</u> up smoking yet.

3. In many of the college classes I am taking now, I <u>met</u> a lot of students who parents pressure them to do well in school, but I think that parental pressure can backfire. I <u>saw</u> several students who <u>became</u> depressed or abused drugs or alcohol when they <u>have not meet</u> their parents' expectations. In contrast, since elementary school, my parents <u>did not pressure</u> me to perform well. Instead, they <u>allowed</u> me to develop my own interests so that I would gradually motivate myself.

Practice Writing Negative Present Perfect Sentences

With a partner, write three present perfect negative sentences expressing something you or someone you know has not done.

e.g.   *I have not learned much grammar until now.*

   Gino has not known his fiancé for long.

1. _____

2. _____

3. _____

Forming Questions in the Present Perfect Tense

Read each of the following sentences and observe how a question is formed in the present perfect tense.

I *have seen* Mr. Rush.

Have you *seen* Mr. Rush?

You *have withdrawn* money from that account.

Have you *withdrawn* money from that account?

She *has criticized* him before.

Has she *criticized* him before?

We *have taken* that route before.

Have you *taken* that route before?

Those teenagers *have eaten* everything.

Have those *teenagers eaten* everything?

A question is formed in the present perfect tense by inserting:

a. the *subject*, the auxiliary verb *has/have*, and the *simple form of the verb.* e.g. *She has spoke?*

b. the auxiliary verb *have or has*, the *subject* of the sentence, ant the *past participle* of the verb. e.g. *Has she spoken?*

c. inserting the auxiliary verb *have or has*, the *subject* and *past tense* of the verb. e.g. *Has she spoke?*

d. all of these

Answer [20]

Forming Questions in the Present Perfect Tense

A question is formed in the present perfect tense by inverting or switching subject and the auxiliary verb has or have.

e.g. I *have sung* before.
    Have you *sung* before?

You *have wasted* too much time.
Have I *wasted* too much time?

Maria *has met* him.
Has Maria *met* him?

We *have had* time to call her.
Have you *had* time to call her?

They *have walked* the dog.
Have they *walked* the dog?

Controlled Practice

Convert each present perfect sentence into a question.

1. They have lived in Chicago since 2006.

---

[20] If you selected choice <u>b</u>, you are correct.

2. She has changed jobs countless times.

_____

3. I have paid her expenses for years.

_____

4. My sister and I have attended the meetings.

_____

5. That dog has chewed up several books.

_____

6. You have asked her to help you in the past.

_____

7. I have been awake most of the night.

_____

8. We have lost interest in that television program.

_____

9. Patricia and Carl have ignored my complaints.

_____

10. That bread has become stale.

_____

Practice Writing Questions

With a partner, write three present perfect questions that you would like to ask someone in your class. But be careful to use the correct meaning of the present perfect tense.

e.g.　　*Has our professor been married before?*

　　　　How long has Gianna known Sergio?

1. _____

2. _____

3. _____

More Error Analysis

Read each of the following short paragraphs and determine if the underlined words use the present perfect and past tenses correctly. If an incorrect tense is used, revise it according to the rules learned in this chapter.

1. Lorena <u>moved</u> from Argentina to San Diego last year. Since that time, she <u>lived</u> with her cousin in a small apartment. It <u>has taken</u> her a long time to adjust to this country and the culture because she <u>had</u> to improve her English skills a lot. However, since she <u>started</u> to work and attend college, she <u>met</u> many people, and they <u>helped</u> her with the different problems she <u>encountered</u> since she moved here.

2. Alana and Tomas <u>toured</u> Northern Europe many times, but they <u>never traveled</u> to Greece. Yesterday, they <u>have decided</u> to plan a trip there. They had originally planned a July vacation, but they <u>revised</u> their plans because they were told that it is very hot there in July.

3. My sister <u>was always</u> very generous with her children, so she <u>decided</u> to give her youngest daughter a special college graduation present. Sarita <u>has never went</u> anywhere, so she wants to take a vacation. Since Sara <u>studied</u> Spanish for years, she wants to go to Colombia so that she can practice her Spanish. To get the best travel package, Sarita and her mother <u>visited</u> many different travel websites to find the best deal.

4. After Houssain <u>arrived</u> in this country, he <u>enrolled</u> in a local college and <u>has</u> <u>graduated</u> a few years later. Since his graduation, he <u>worked</u> for a computer company, and <u>remained</u> at this company for several reasons. The first is that his employer is paying for his master's degree. The second reason is that he likes his job and the people with whom he works. If Houssain wanted, he could get another job that pays a lot more, but he <u>decided</u> to stay in this company for the time being because it is a satisfying job and environment.

More Practice Writing

1. Write a paragraph describing activities you have participated in for the past five or ten years. These topics could include religious, family, school, or social activities.

2. Write a paragraph describing two activities you have participated in many times such as going to your church, eating in a certain restaurant, visiting someone in a hospital, going to the local public library, etc.

3. Recall an event that occurred at an unknown time in your early childhood. Then write a paragraph about this occasion.

The Past Perfect Tense

- The goal of this chapter is to explain the form and the meaning of the past perfect tense.

The Meaning of the Past Perfect Tense

Read the following sentences and place the number **1** above the action that occurred first and the number **2** above action that occurred second.

                                              2   **1**
e.g. Before the basketball game <u>started,</u> I <u>had finished</u> my homework.

1. Juan Carlos <u>indicated</u> that he <u>had spoken</u> to Alicia previously.

2. As soon as Anna <u>had fallen</u> asleep, the alarm clock <u>rang</u>.

3. We <u>had waited</u> for over an hour, when doctor finally <u>arrived.</u>

4. I <u>mentioned</u> to Elvira that Henrick <u>had telephoned</u> me.

The tense labeled number 1 is the:

    a. present perfect tense.

    b. past perfect tense.

    c. simple past tense

    d. simple present tense.

Answer [1]

The tense labeled number 2 is called the:

    a. present perfect tense.

    b. past perfect tense.

    c. simple past tense

    d. simple present tense.

Answer [2]

---

[1] If you selected choice <u>b</u>, you are correct.
[2] If you selected choice <u>c</u>, you are correct.

The past perfect tense indicates that:

  a. two actions occurred in the distant past.

  b. the action expressed in the past perfect tense occurred recently.

  c. the action expressed in the past tense occurred after the action in the past perfect tense.

  d. a and b

Answer [3]

Read the following sentences and note tense used in each.

  a. By that time, I <u>had called</u> Mariska many times.

  b. They <u>had encountered</u> computer problems before.

  c. The professor <u>had taught</u> that class previously.

In these sentences, the writer used the past perfect tense because:

  a. only one action occurred.

  b. a past time was suggested or implied.

  c. it would have been confusing.

  d. it sounded right.

Answer [4]

Read each of the following sentences.

  a. You had <u>never</u> lied until that time.

  b. He had <u>already</u> called his mother earlier that day.

  c. By that time, I had <u>just</u> finished my class.

The part of speech of the <u>underlined</u> word is:

  a. noun

  b. verb

  c. adjective

  d. adverb

  e. preposition

Answer [5]

---

[3] If you selected choice <u>c</u>, you are correct.
[4] If you selected choice <u>b</u>, you are correct.
[5] If you selected choice <u>d</u>, you are correct.

An adverb was inserted in these sentences to:

    a. give emphasis or clarity.

    b. justify the use of the past perfect.

    c. make the sentence less boring.

    d. all of these.

Answer [6]

Which of the following adverbs could be used with the past perfect tense?

    a. yet

    b. never

    c. already

    d. just

    e. all of these

Answer [7]

The Meaning of the Past Perfect Tense

The past perfect tense is used when discussing two different past events. The past perfect is used to describe the action that occurred first, while the simple past is used to describe the more recent action.

action that occurred first ↓	action that occurred second ↓

e.g. We <u>had eaten</u> dinner when my sister finally <u>arrived.</u>

The past perfect tense can be used when a past time is implied or suggested.

e.g. We had seen that man **before.**
      I had bought furniture from that store **in the past.**

The adverbs *already, never, just,* and *yet* are frequently used in the past perfect tense to give emphasis.

e.g. Filipo had **never** used a computer until then.
      Ahmed had **just** called his parents that morning.

---

[6] If you selected choice <u>a</u>, you are correct.
[7] If you selected choice <u>e</u>, you are correct.

84

Forming the Past Perfect Tense

I <u>had called</u> her frequently.　　　　We <u>had solved</u> similar problems before.

You <u>had been</u> sick before that time.

That child <u>had talked</u> to me earlier.

The teacher <u>had complained</u> before.　　They <u>had been</u> kind to her for all those years.

That dog <u>had barked</u> previously.

Can you create a rule for forming the past perfect tense?

<u>subject +</u> _____ + _____

Answer [8]

Try to write a sentence using the past perfect.

_____

With the past perfect tense, you can also use contractions. Select the correct contractions from the following choices.

a.　I had = I'd　　　　　　　　f.　　we had = we'd
b.　you had = you'd
c.　he had = he'd
d.　she had = she'd　　　　　　g.　　they had = they'd
e.　all of these

Answer [9]

Select the correct rule if you intend to include an adverb in the past perfect.

a.　subject + adverb + present tense of have (had) + past participle e.g. *I already have eaten.*

b.　subject + past tense of have (had) + adverb + present participle e.g. *I had just eating.*

c.　subject + past tense of have (had) + adverb + past participle e.g. *I had just eaten.*

d.　none of these

Answer [10]

---

[8] Subject + past tense of have (had) + the past participle
[9] If you selected choice <u>e</u>, you are correct.
[10] If you selected choice <u>c</u>, you are correct

Controlled Practice

In a small group, read the sentence, and complete it with either the simple past or the past perfect tense. If an adverb is included be certain to follow the rule just learned to position it correctly.

1. Before I (meet) _____ my husband, I (be) _____ sad and

    lonely.

2. When Susana's parents (arrive) _____ home, the party (end, already)

    _____ .

3. We (finish, just) _____ dinner, when my nephew (call)

    _____ to ask for help.

4. You (be, never) _____ to Florida before that time.

5. My cousins (study) _____ English for ten years, before they

   (move) _____ to the United States.

6. Alta-Gracia (work) _____ part time in a bank, before she (complete)

   _____ her college degree.

7. Carlos and Julisa (fall, just) _____ asleep, when their phone (ring)

   _____.

8. Raj and I (encounter, never) _____ such a fascinating person

   until that time.

9. Anna and Pedro (spend, already) _____ all their savings on a

   new car, when their daughter (announce) _____ that she needed

   money to pay her tuition.

10. You (tell) _____ my boss that I (be already) _____

    late several times.

Controlled Practice

With a partner, combine the following sentences pairs using the simple past tense and the past perfect tense. You can re-arrange or omit words, and you can make one sentence a dependent clause by using subordinating conjunctions such as when, after, before, until, as soon as, etc.

e.g.   At midnight Janina was asleep. At 2:00 AM she woke up when a dog barked.

   Janina had been asleep for two hours, when a dog barked and woke her up. or
   A dog barked and woke up Janina after she had already been asleep for 2 hours.

1. Mrs. Cuervo left for work. Two hours later, her husband tried to call her.

   _____

   _____

2. Our class began at 12 o'clock noon. John walked in the door at 12:30.

   _____

   _____

3. We ate dinner at 6 o'clock. My friends arrived at 7:30.

   _____

   _____

4. Larisa left for work at 6:30 AM. I rang her doorbell at 7 AM.

   _____

   _____

5. Tran lived in Vietnam his entire life. He moved to New York last year.

   _____

   _____

6. The professor asked a question. The students knew the answer immediately.

   _____

   _____

7. In 2009, Marco and Paolo started medical school. They graduated from college with honors in 2008.

   _____

   _____

8. Marta began to work on Wall Street in January. She met Manual in March.

   _____

   _____

9. You missed many classes. Then, your teacher threatened to fail you.

   _____

   _____

10. He treated me poorly at the meeting. I didn't want to work with him after this incident.

_____

_____

Practice in Context

Discussion

Before reading this article entitled, *How victim snared ID thief: She chased down woman who had given her 6 months of hell*, as a class discuss:

- **what identity theft is**
- **how a person's identity can be stolent and**
- **specify the types of problems it creates.**

Reading Completing the Passage with the Correct Tense

Read the following article that appeared on June 15, 2007 in San Francisco Chronicle, and complete each blank with either the past or past perfect tense. Remember when you use the past perfect tense, you must be referencing two activities that occurred at different times in the past so that the older event is expressed in the past perfect tense.

If it hadn't been for the distinctive suede coat, there would have been no chase through the streets of San Francisco, no heroine and, in all likelihood, no justice. But when Karen Lodrick (turn) _____ away from ordering her latte at the Starbucks at Church and Market streets, there it (be) _____, slung over the arm of the woman behind her.

It was, Lodrick thought, a "beaucoup expensive" light-brown suede coat with faux fur trim at the collar, cuffs and down the middle. The only other time Lodrick, a 41-year-old creative consultant, (see) _____ that particular coat (be) _____ on a security camera photo that her bank, Wells Fargo, showed her of the woman who (steal) _____ her identity. The photo was taken as the thief was looting Lodrick's checking account.

Now, here (be) _____ the coat again. This woman, a big woman, about 5 feet 10, maybe 150 pounds, (have) _____ to be the person who (put) _____ her through six months of hell and (cost) _____ her $30,000 in lost business as she (try) _____ to untangle the never-ending mess with banks and credit agencies.

Lodrick's heart was pounding. Despite the expensive coat, the Prada bag, the glitter-frame Gucci glasses, there (be) _____ something not right about the impostor she would later learn was named Maria Nelson. "She (have) _____ bad teeth and (look) _____ like she (bathe) _____," the onetime standup comic recalled recently. "I thought, 'You're buying Prada on my dime. Go get your teeth fixed.' "

When Nelson got up to leave, Lodrick, who is 5 feet 2 and 110 pounds but comes from what she calls "a fighting family," made an instant decision. First she (call) _____ 911. Then she (follow) _____ Nelson down Market Street. The foot chase was on.

Nelson (turn) _____ up Buchanan Street in front of the new San Francisco Mint with Lodrick after her. Lodrick (feel) _____ an almost otherwordly calm and (be) _____ entirely focused on not losing sight of this person who (make) _____ her feel so unsafe. Meanwhile, she was giving the 911 operator a play-by-play on her cell phone.

She didn't really know what she would do if she caught Nelson. "She was a big girl," Lodrick recalled. She (tell) _____ the 911 operator she (feel) _____ a little scared. The operator said: "If you in any way feel threatened, do not continue the pursuit."

Lodrick (tell) _____ the operator: "No, I'm OK."

Back on Market Street, Nelson (hail) _____ a cab. Lodrick (run) _____ up to the cabbie: "I have 911 on the line," she told him. "Please don't drive away. I think she's stealing my identity." The driver (lift) _____ his hands off the steering wheel in a gesture that said he would stay put. Nelson (jump) _____ out of the cab.

"Stop following me," she beseeched Lodrick. "You're scaring me."

"I'm scared, too," Lodrick answered. "Let's just wait for the police, and we can straighten this out."

"I can't," Nelson said. "I'm on probation."

Indeed, court records show that Nelson (be) _____ on probation for one of eight previous fraud convictions and also (be) _____ convicted of theft. Later, the San Francisco police detective who worked the case, Bruce Fairbairn, said Nelson's statement about probation, relayed to the 911 operator by Lodrick, was a key to extracting a guilty plea.

Nelson (take) _____ off again. In front of West Coast Growers, she (drop) _____ a wallet into an abandoned shopping cart. Lodrick, still after her, picked up the wallet -- also Prada -- and found an entire set of identification, including credit cards, a Social Security card and a debit card all in the name of Karen Lodrick. Later, when she (return) _____ to the bank that (be) _____ her original destination that morning and took possession of the lost driver's license, it (be) _____ a perfect forgery -- with a hologram and a California seal -- and it (have) _____ Lodrick's name but Nelson's photo and physical characteristics.

When Officer Rickey Terrell (arrive) _____ a moment later -- about 45 minutes after the chase began -- he, too, searched the Walgreens garage. He (find) _____ Nelson crouched behind a car smoking a cigarette in front of an emergency exit.

A relieved Lodrick laughed out loud, surprising herself. "You idiot," she said to Nelson. "You should have run."

One unexpected outcome of having her identity stolen is that Lodrick was invited to become a San Francisco cop by Fairbairn, the inspector who handled the case.

"She's quite the detective," he said. "I was so impressed by her courage, her dogged determination and her savvy that I (take) _____ her down to recruitment. She has the best natural instincts for a cop I've seen in years."

Lodrick's experience did give her an appetite for fighting crime. But in the end, she decided, "I just don't have the stomach for it."

Negation: Making the Past Perfect Tense Negative

Read each of the following sentences and observe how the past perfect tense is made negative.

I *had not seen* her yet.

You *had not planned* to be absent.

She *had not called* him before.

He *had not been* dishonest previously.

This information *had not emerged* earlier.

We *had not been* to Egypt until that time.

The parents *had not complained* about that teacher in the past.

The past perfect tense is made negative by inserting the subject:

a. the auxiliary verb *had*, the word *not*, and the *past participle*. e.g. She *had not eaten* yet.

b. the auxiliary verb *have or has*, the word *not* and the *present participle* of the verb. e.g. She *has not eating* yet.

c. the auxiliary verb *had*, the word *not* and *past tense* of the verb. e.g. She *had not ate* yet.

d. none of these

Answer [11]

When the past perfect tense is negative, you can also use contractions, as in the following examples.

I *hadn't visited* many countries yet.

You *hadn't told* her yet.

He *hadn't discussed* it previously.

She *hadn't asked* many questions.

It *hadn't snowed* for years.

We *hadn't traveled* much until that time.

Those men *hadn't cooperated* in the past.

---

[11] If you selected choice a, you are correct.

The Negative Form of the Past Perfect Tense

The past perfect tense is made negative by using the following rule:

e.g. I *had not swum* before then.   We *had not written* to her for ages.
You *had not drunk* much soda.
Maria *had not yelled* at him.   They *had not neglected* her before.

You can also use contractions in the past perfect tense, as in the following examples.

e.g. I *hadn't waited* for hours.   We *hadn't earned* enough money.
You *hadn't heard* the news yet.
Mara *hadn't scolded* him before.   They *hadn't discussed* marriage prior to this time.

Controlled Practice

Make each underlined past perfect verb negative.

1. They <u>had worked</u> in a factory prior to 2001.

    _____

2. Chang and his wife <u>had changed</u> doctors by that time.

    _____

3. I <u>had assisted</u> her many times before that incident.

    _____

4. My uncle and I <u>had just cleaned</u> the house when they arrived.

    _____

5. That cat <u>had scratched</u> the furniture previously.

    _____

6. You <u>had paid</u> her credit card bills many times.

    _____

7. I <u>had slept</u> very well until the car alarm sounded.

8. They <u>had become</u> tired of her constant complaining by that time.

_____

9. Paola and Carla <u>had argued</u> many times prior to that incident.

_____

10. That cake <u>had become</u> stale and hard.

_____

Practice Writing Negative Past Perfect Sentences

With a partner, write five past perfect negative sentences expressing something that Karen Lodrick hadn't done or been involved in before her identity theft ordeal. Remember when you use the past perfect tense, you must be referencing two activities that occurred at different times in the past so that the older event is expressed in the past perfect tense.

e.g.   *Karen Lodrick had not seen the light-brown suede coat until she saw the security camera video.*

         Karen Lodrick had not been in that bank branch before that time.

1. _____

2. _____

3. _____

4. _____

5. _____

Forming Questions in the Past Perfect Tense

Read each of the following sentences and observe how a question is formed in the past perfect tense.

I *had left* for work by then.
Had you *left* for work by then?

We *had debated* this issue previously.
Had you *debated* this issue previously?

You *had spent* hours chatting by that time.
Had I *spent* hours chatting by that time?

His mother *had corrected* him before.
Had his mother *corrected* him before?

Those children *had played* tennis for years.
Had those children *played* tennis for years?

A question is formed in the past perfect tense by inserting:

   a.   the *subject*, the auxiliary verb *had*, and the *simple form of the verb.* e.g. *He had steal* credit cards before?

   b.   the auxiliary verb *had*, the *subject* of the sentence, and the *past participle* of the verb. e.g. *Had he stolen* credit cards before?

   c.   inserting the auxiliary verb *had*, the *subject* and *past tense* of the verb. e.g. *Had he stole* credit cards before?

   d.   inserting the auxiliary verb *has or have*, the *subject* and *past participle* of the verb. e.g. *Has he stolen* credit cards before?

Answer [12]

Forming Questions in the Past Perfect Tense

A question is formed in the past perfect tense by inverting or switching the subject and the auxiliary verb had.

e.g. I *had called* earlier.
      Had you *called* earlier?

We *had played* cards before.
Had you *played* cards before?

You *had broken* the rules previously.
Had I *broken* the rules previously?

Erico *had met* her years ago.
Had Erico *met* her years ago?

They *had cleaned* the house.
Had they *cleaned* the house?

Controlled Practice

Convert each <u>underlined</u> past perfect verb into a question.

1. Stephen King <u>had written</u> many books before his accident.

---

[12] If you selected choice <u>b</u>, you are correct.

2. The deer had fled before we could help him.

_____

3. We had tolerated her nonsense for years.

_____

4. I had dealt with computer viruses in the past.

_____

5. That picture had disappeared years before I noticed it.

_____

6. You had expressed your disapproval in the past.

_____

7. I had already spoken by the time he arrived.

_____

8. Joseph had lost interest in Clara by that time.

_____

9. Pietro and Carl had opened up several stores previously.

_____

10. The information in that medical book had become outdated.

_____

Practice Writing Questions

With a partner, write three past perfect questions about Karen Lodrick, Maria Nelson or the police officials involved in this case. Remember when you use the past perfect tense, you must be referencing two activities that occurred at different times in the past so that the older event is expressed in the past perfect tense.

e.g.   *Had Maria Nelson ever been arrested before this incident?*

Had Karen Lodrick worked as a police officer previously?

1. _____

2. _____

3. _____

4. _____

5. _____

Practice Writing

Part One:

Complete the following chart specifying the activities that Karen Lodrick engaged in to catch the woman who had stolen her identity.

1.	
2.	
3.	
4.	
5.	
6.	
7.	
8	
9.	
10.	

Part Two

Use the chart just created to write five sentences using the simple past and the past perfect tenses to describe activities that Karen Lodrick, Maria Nelson or the police had completed before another incident occurred.

e.g. *In Starbuck's, Karen Lodrick* **remembered** *that she* **had seen** *the unusual suede coat on the video tap.*

Lodrick **noticed** *that Nelson* **hadn't had** *her teeth fixed, even though she was dressed in very expensive clothes.*

1. _____

2. _____

3. _____

4. _____

5. _____

Error Analysis

Read the following paragraph and make any corrections in the use of the underlined simple past and past perfect verbs.

While Karen Lodrick was standing on line in Starbucks, she <u>had noticed</u> a woman in a very unusual and expensive outfit. Even though the woman was wearing very luxurious clothing, Karen <u>had sensed</u> that the woman <u>hadn't taken</u> a shower for quite some time. Karen also <u>noted</u> that the woman <u>hadn't seen</u> a dentist in ages because her teeth were in such bad shape. Suddenly, Karen <u>realized</u> that she <u>had saw</u> this woman before. Her name <u>was</u> Maria Nelson. Karen <u>saw</u> her in a security video after Nelson <u>pilfered</u> Karen's checking account. As Nelson began to leave Starbucks, Karen <u>decided</u> to follow her, but she first called 911 for assistance. Karen <u>pursued</u> Nelson by herself for almost forty-five minutes before an officer <u>arrived</u>, and <u>caught</u> Nelson hiding in a Waldgreen's garage. After the police officer <u>had captured</u> Nelson, Karen <u>told</u> Nelson that she <u>was</u> an idiot for not running away. As a result of Karen's keen, responsible detective instincts, Inspector Fairbairn, who handled the case, has invited Karen to become a San Francisco police officer, although Karen has graciously turned down his offer.

More Practice Writing

Write about one of the following topics.

1. Write a paragraph describing a time when you or someone you know had something personal stolen such as a credit card, wallet, cash, jewelry. Describe what occurred and how you responded after the incident.

2. Write a composition describing a time you or someone you know became a victim of identity theft.

Remember when you use the past perfect tense, you must be referencing two activities that occurred at different times in the past so that the older event is expressed in the past perfect tense.

The Future Tense

- The goal of this chapter is to teach you to understand and use the future tense accurately.

The Meaning of the Future Tense

The future tense is used to:

1. volunteer or express a willingness to help;

2. make predictions about the future; and

3. express a preconceived plan.

The next three sections will explain these uses in detail.

1. Using "*will*" to Volunteer or Offer Help

Read each pair of sentences, and answer the questions below.

a. I <u>will help</u> you set up your computer.

b You <u>will prepare</u> the sandwiches.

c. Gita <u>will take</u> the children to the park.

d. Sana <u>will write</u> the invitations to the party.

e. We <u>will order</u> tables and chairs.

f. Enrico and Marisa <u>will decorate</u> the house.

What tense is used in each sentence?

a. the simple present tense

b. the present perfect tense

c. the future tense

d. the past perfect tense

Answer [1]

The future tense is used in these sentences to:

a. demonstrate the completion of an act.

b. express a willingness to do something.

c. to volunteer to help.

---

[1] If you selected choice <u>c</u>, you are correct.

d.   b and c

2.   Using *to be going to* or *will* to make predictions

a.   Read each sentence, and answer the questions below.

  a.   I will graduate from high school this year.

  b   You will become a nurse in two years.

  c.   Sara will succeed at her job.

  d.   Bao will win a million dollars in the lottery.

  e.   We will save enough money to buy a house.

  f.   Tomas and Pietro will pass their driver's test the first time.

In the six sentences above, the future tense is used to:

  a.   volunteer or offer help.

  b.   express a past situation or event.

  c.   make predictions about the future.

  d.   express a continuous situation.

Answer [3]

b.   Read each sentences, and answer the questions below.

  a.   I am going to improve my writing.

  b   You are going to be a wonderful teacher.

  c.   Jean is going to perform well at her job.

  d.   Louis is going to get rich playing the stock market.

  e.   We are going to purchase a new car.

  f.   They are going to miss the bus.

---

[2] If you selected choice <u>d</u>, you are correct.
[3] If you selected choice <u>c</u>, you are correct.

What meaning does the expression *to be going to* state in these sentences?

a. the present tense

b. the future tense

c. the present progressive tense

d. past tense

Answer [4]

In the previous six sentences, the expression *to be going to* can be used to:

a. volunteer or offer help.

b. make predictions about the future

c. express a present time event.

d. express a continuous situation.

Answer [5]

3. Using "*to be going to*" to Express a Preconceived Plan

Read each sentence, and answer the questions below.

a. I <u>am going to take</u> a tour of Egypt in January.

b   You <u>are going to major</u> in chemistry.

c. Sara <u>is going to register</u> for 18 credits.

d. Barbara <u>is going to marry</u> Sergio in the spring.

e. We <u>are going to watch</u> the baby on Monday.

f. Those young men <u>are going to set up</u> my new television.

In these sentences, the future tense is used to:

a. volunteer or offer help.

b. express a present time event.

c. make predictions about the future.

d. express a preconceived plan.

e. a and b

Answer [6]

---

[4] If you selected choice <u>b</u>, you are correct.
[5] If you selected choice <u>b</u>, you are correct.
[6] If you selected choice <u>d</u>, you are correct.

Forming the Future Tense

Read the following chart, and observe how the future tense is formed.

I will donate blood.   We will name the baby Clarissa.
I am going to donate blood.   We are going to name the baby Clarissa.

You will graduate soon.
You are going to graduate soon.

Sarita will purchase a computer.   They will lose all their money gambling.
Sarita is going to buy a computer.   They are going to lose all their money gambling.

In how many ways, can the future tense be expressed?

   a. one

   b. two

   c. three

   d. four

Answer [7]

---

[7] If you selected choice b, you are correct.

Select the rule(s) that state the two forms of the future tense. After the subject, insert:

   a.   the modal, *will* plus the *simple form of the verb*. e.g. We *will discuss* the problem.

   b.   the present tense of *to be going to* and the *simple form of the verb*. e.g. We *are going to discuss* the problem. I *am going to discuss* the problem.

   c.   the modal would plus the *simple form of the verb*. e.g. We *would discuss* the problem.

   d.   the past tense of *to be going to* and the *simple form of the verb*. e.g. We *were going to discuss* the problem.

   e.   a and b.

Answer [8]

In future tense, you can also insert an adverb between the auxiliary verb (will) and the simple verb. Observe the following examples.

I *will **also** arrive* early.   We *will **never** lie* to our parents.

You *will **just** have* to wait.

He *will **hardly even** speak* a word.

She *will **rarely*** complain.   They *will **already** know* the answer.

That dog *will **always** bark.*

When *to be going to* expresses a future tense, you can insert an adverb between the auxiliary verb (are) and the present participle (going). Observe the following examples.

I *am **also** going to study* harder.   We *are **never** going to give* up.

You *are **just** going to be* frustrated.

He *is **barely even** going to pass* the class.

She *is **already** going* to call her.   They *are **constantly** going to complain.*

That dog *is **always** going to beg* for food.

---

[8] If you selected choice e, you are correct.

Forming Future Tense

The future tense can be formed in two different ways.

1. **The modal *will* can be used to express a preconceived plan, or a willingness to help or volunteer.**

    e.g.   I *will speak* to him.   We *will obey* the laws.
           You *will improve* your baking.
           Maria *will listen* to me.   They *will assist* her.

    An adverb can also be inserted between the auxiliary verb (will) and the simple verb, as in the following examples.

    e.g.   I *will **also** look* for him.   We *will **never** know* why.
           You *will **always** dislike* her.
           Maria *will **rarely** think of* her.   They *will **frequently** criticize* her.

2. **The expression *to be going to* can be used to express a preconceived plan or to make a prediction by using the following rule.**

    e.g.   I *am going to enjoy* this show.   We *are going to send* a gift.
           You *are going to waste* my time.
           She *is going to accept* the job.   They *are going to drink* milk.

    An adverb can also be inserted after the verb *to be (am, is, are)* and before *going to* such as in the following examples.

    e.g.   I *am **also** going* to leave early.   We *are **never** going to cry.*
           You *are **never** going to quit.*
           It *is **rarely** going to occur.*   They *are **always** going to object.*

Controlled Practice

Complete each of the following sentences with the correct form of the future tense.

1. Maria wants to help you prepare for the holiday meal. Therefore, she (arrive)

    _____ at your house early, and she (assist) _____ you in

    preparing the meal.

2. Mohammed knows how to invest money wisely, and is very cautious with his

    investments, so he (become) _____ wealthy someday.

3. Some of my girlfriends don't want to have careers. Instead, they (search constantly) _____ for very rich, good looking guys to marry them because they say they want to be traditional housewives. I wonder if they (be) _____ happy.

4. Her grandparents are planning a special trip to celebrate their fiftieth wedding anniversary. They (travel) _____ on a big fancy cruise ship. Their ship (leave) _____ from New York. Next, It (dock) _____ in several large cities in Spain, Greece, and Egypt, and they (tour) _____ these cities during the day, but at night (return) _____ to their cruise ship to sleep. This trip (be) _____ very costly, but they have saved their money for years, and they are looking forward to their voyage.

5. After I graduate from college next year, I (take definitely) _____ off the whole summer. In fact, I (sleep) _____ late everyday. At night, I (go) _____ out with my friends to clubs. Finally, at the end of the summer, I (search reluctantly) _____ for a job. In contrast, my girlfriend (take) _____ a trip, and she (visit) _____ London first. Next, she (board) _____ a ferry to travel to France. Then she (take) _____ a train to Paris, and (stay) _____ in a pension for several days. Since she has a limited amount of money, she (take) _____ stand by flights. This can be very inconvenient, but it (save definitely) _____ her lots of money on her airfare. Once she returns home, she (have also) _____ to look for a full time job, too. Because her degree is in finance, she thinks that she (search) _____ for a job in the banking industry.

Practice Writing

1. Write a couple of sentences volunteering to help someone in a special situation.

e.g. *I will help my mother prepare for the holidays. Before I arrive, I will bake some cookies and cakes. The day before the holiday, I will clean her house. After the meal, I will scrub all the pots, pans and dishes, and I will clean up the house after the guests leave.*

_____
_____
_____
_____
_____

2. Write a couple of sentences describing a preconceived plan you have.

e.g. *On Tuesday, I am going to get up at five o'clock and eat a big breakfast because I will be out until late that evening. Then I am going to take the train to Washington to meet with the president. After I meet him, I will visit some of the historic places in Washington. Finally, I am going to return home on the shuttle.*

_____
_____
_____
_____
_____
_____
_____

3. Write a paragraph making predictions about the future of some of the people in your class.

e.g. *Sadaf will be very successful because she is diligent and smart. However, Atif is not going to do as well because he can never arrive on time, and he forgets to do his homework. If he is always late or forgets to do his work, his boss will get very angry, and he will fire him.*

_____
_____
_____
_____
_____

Negation: Making the Future Tense Negative

Read the following chart, and observe how the future tense is made negative when the modal *will* is used.

I will marry her.
I <u>will not marry</u> her.
I <u>won't marry</u> her.

We will telephone my sister.
We <u>will not telephone</u> my sister.
We <u>won't telephone</u> my sister.

You will leave early.
You <u>will not leave</u> early.
You <u>won't leave</u> early.

Sana will buy a car this year.
Sana <u>will not buy</u> a car this year.
Sana <u>won't buy</u> a car this year.

They will win the game.
They <u>will not win</u> the game.
They <u>won't win</u> the game.

Can you complete the rule for making the future tense negative when the modal *will* is used?

<u>**Subject** +</u> _____ + _____ + <u>**simple form of the verb**</u>

Answer [9]

When the writer contracts the words will and not, what contraction can be used?

   a. wouldn't

   b. won't

   c. willn't

   d. none of these

Answer [10]

Try to write a sentence using this rule.

_____

---

[9] subject + will + not + simple form of the verb *or*
   subject + won't + simple form of the verb
[10] If you selected <u>b</u>, you are correct

Read the following chart, and observe how the future tense is made negative when the expression *to be going to* is used.

I <u>am not going to write</u> a book.
I<u>'m not going to write</u> a book

We <u>are not going to drive</u> into the city.
We<u>'re not going to drive</u> into the city.
We <u>aren't going to drive</u> into the city.

You <u>are not going to give</u> me a soda.
You <u>aren't going to give</u> me a soda.
You<u>'re not going to give</u> me a soda.

She <u>is not going to complain</u> again.
She <u>isn't going to complain</u> again.
She<u>'s not going to complain</u> again.

They <u>are not going to work</u> this weekend.
They <u>aren't going to work</u> this weekend.
They<u>'re not going to work</u> this weekend.

Can you write the rule for making the future tense negative when the phrase *to be going to* is used?

subject + _____ + not + _____ + simple form of the verb

Answer [11]

What contraction can be used when the expression *to be going to* is used?

    a. I'm not

    b. aren't

    c. isn't

    d. all of these

Answer [12]

Try to write a sentence using this rule.

_____

---

[11] subject + present tense to be (am, is or are) + not + going to + simple form of the verb and you can also use contractions as demonstrated in the chart.
[12] If you selected choice <u>d</u>, you are correct

The Negative Form of the Future Tense

1. **When the modal *will* is used, the future tense is made negative by inserting the word *not* after the word *will*.**

   e.g. I *will **not** work* with them.   We *will **not** disobey* the rules.
         You *will **not** understand*.
         She *will **not** yell* at me.   They *will **not** lie*.

You can also use contractions with the future tense, as demonstrated in the following examples.

   e.g. I ***won't** yell* at him.   We ***won't** break* the laws.
         You ***won't** wait* for me.
         She ***won't** stop* me.   They ***won't** eat* fish.

2. **The expression *to be going to* is made negative by inserting the word *not* after the auxiliary verb *am, is* or *are*.**

   e.g. I *am **not** going to leave* early.   We *are **not** going to write* a letter.
         You *are **not** going to be* sick.
         She *is **not** going to practice*.   They *are **not** going to* return late.

You can also use contractions with the expression *to be going to* as in the following examples.

   e.g. *I'm not going to* fail.   *We're not going to* miss class.
         You *aren't going to* smoke.
         She *isn't going to* be early.   They *aren't going to* go home.

Controlled Practice

With a partner, make the following future tense sentences negative.

1. Amy and Chang will get engaged soon.

   _____

2. They are going to run ten miles.

   _____

3. Rebecca and Kate will call us soon.

   _____

4. My husband and I are going to redecorate the house.

    _____

5. I am going to decide by next week.

    _____

6. You are going to be defeated.

    _____

7. He will call his father for advice.

    _____

8. The doctors are going to recommend heart surgery.

    _____

9. They will rent an apartment in this town.

    _____

10. You will learn to park a car in a small space.

    _____

Writing

1. Use *to be going to* or *will* to predict three reasons why social networking websites like MySpace.com and Facebook will change how people interact in the future.

    e.g.   *Facebook is going to permit more people to stay in contact even if they don't live near each other.*

1. _____

    _____

2. _____

    _____

3. _____

    _____

2. Use *to be going to* or *will* to predict three reasons why social networking sites such as MySpace.com and Facebook will not be beneficial.

e.g.   *Social network sites **won't demand** that their users be truthful so that many people will lie to each other.*

1. _____

_____

2. _____

_____

3. _____

_____

3. Use the future tense to explain how parents, school, libraries and teachers can reduce some of the problems that have arisen because of social networking websites.

e.g.   *High schools **will reduce** problems if their computers are blocked from accessing websites such as Myspace.com.*

1. _____

_____

2. _____

_____

3. _____

_____

Forming Questions in the Future Tense

Read the following chart, and observe how a question in formed in the future tense when the modal *will* is used.

I <u>will call</u> the doctor.
<u>Will you call</u> the doctor?

We <u>will clean</u> the apartment.
<u>Will you clean</u> the apartment?

You <u>will improve</u> your writing.
<u>Will I improve</u> my writing?

Sana <u>will watch</u> the baby.
<u>Will Sana watch</u> the baby?

They <u>will lose</u> the game.
<u>Will they lose</u> the game?

Can you complete the rule for making the future tense negative when the modal *will* is used?

Will _____ + _____ + _____ **?**

Answer [13]

Try to write a question using this rule.

Read the following chart, and observe how the future tense is formed when the expression *to be going to* is used.

I <u>am going to call</u> a doctor.   We <u>are going to bring</u> some candy.
<u>Are you going to call</u> a doctor?   <u>Are you going to</u> bring some candy?

You <u>are going to listen.</u>
<u>Am I going to listen</u>?

Sudir <u>is going to watch</u> the show.   They <u>are going to rest</u>.
<u>Is Sudir going to watch</u> the show?   <u>Are they going to rest</u>?

Can you write the rule for forming a question in the future tense when the phrase *to be going to* is used?

| **present tense** | | | **simple form** |
| **to be (am, is, are)** + | _____ + | _____ + | **of the verb** **?** |

Answer [14]

Try to write a sentence using this rule.

---

[13] Will + subject + simple form of the verb ?
[14] present tense of to be (am, is or are) + subject + going to + simple form of the verb ?

Forming Questions in the Future Tense

1. **When the modal *will* is used, a question in formed in the future tense by inverting or switching the subject with the auxiliary verb *will*.**

    e.g. *Will I buy a car* next year?   *Will Carlo and I graduate* this year?
          Will you marry me?
          Will Sadat be home?   *Will they understand* us?
          Will the dog beg for food?

2. **When the expression *to be going to* is used, a question is formed by inverting or switching the subject with the auxiliary verb am, is or are.**

    e.g. *Am I going to sell* my house?   *Are we going to visit* them?
          Are you going to listen to me?
          Is he going to work tonight?   *Are they going to ask* her?

Controlled Practice

With a partner, convert the following future tense sentences into questions.

1. Marco and Tamara will write an article about the cafeteria.

    _____

2. They are going to travel in Mexico next month.

    _____

3. Reina and I will contact the teachers.

    _____

4. My husband and his sister are going to visit their mother.

    _____

5. We are going to paint my house red.

    _____

6. You are going to be late for class again.

7. He will eat chicken, pasta and salad.

_____

8. The nurses are going to ask for an increase in pay.

_____

9. They will attend the party.

_____

10. You will write a term paper carefully.

_____

Practice Writing

Interview your class members and ask them about their plans for the future. With a partner or in a small group, write six questions asking classmates:

- what they will volunteer to do for their parents, siblings, school, employers, or friends after they graduate from college;
- what plans will they make in the next few years; and
- what they predict will occur in their futures personally, professionally, academically, and financially.

e.g. *Will Estafan offer to support his parents after he graduates?*

Is Erica going to work 60 hours a week?

Will Sudir save enough money to buy a home?

Am I going to write a book someday?

1. _____

2. _____

3. _____

4. _____

5. _____

Error Analysis

Each of the following sentences contains an error in the use of the future tense. Read each sentence carefully and make the necessary revisions so that the future tense is used accurately.

1. If drug addicts aren't going to received the social and emotional support they need, they will continues to abuse drugs.

2. Research has demonstrated that when children enjoy their local library's story hour, they will to read more, and they are going to improved their reading skills.

3. The tutor will pointed out the mistakes, and the student will corrects them.

4. Most parents won't known if their teenagers create secret e-mail addresses.

5. Because the death penalty will had intimidated criminals, it will reduce crime.

6. Asmita's parents going to arranged her marriage?

7. Suspending a student for cheating will be teach cheaters to be honest and responsible.

8. Controlling access to social networking websites will more effective than eliminating them completely.

9. If a punishment is reasonable, the offender won't be reacted irrationally.

10. If a criminal is executed, he will lost the opportunity to redeem himself.

11. If the capital punishment is legalized, will innocent people been executed?

12. Life in prison will not prevents violent crime.

13. My brother will not competitive with other children because he fears failure.

14. Is Silvia going to learns to drive a car?

15. Prohibiting a person from using a cell phone while driving not going to prevent accidents.

Practice Writing Compositions

Write a composition about one of the following topics.

1.   Discuss the plans you and/or a friend have for the future. These plans could include your education, career, and family.

2.   As the principal of a local public high school, you must develop a plan to prevent the students from being victimized in social networking websites when they use the high school's computers. Propose a plan, and predict what the students' reactions to this plan will be. Finally, explain how you will handle their objections.

Modals

In this chapter you will learn how to use modals effectively. Modals express the "mood" of the verb because they communicate probability, possibility, obligation, or necessity.

Which group contains modals?

   a. to be, to see, to go, to do
   b. can, could, will, would, may, might, should, must, ought to
   c. beautiful, ugly, adorable, hateful, loving.
   d. myself, yourselves, himself, herself, ourselves, themselves

Answer [1]

What part of speech must follow a modal?

   a. a past participle (sung)
   b. a verb in the past tense form (sang)
   c. a verb in the simple form (sing)
   d. a present participle (singing)

Answer [2]

The Modal Can

Read the following sentences to determine the meaning of the underlined modal.

   1. Alejandro <u>can speak</u> English, Spanish and Russian.
   2. I <u>can swim</u> one mile in the ocean.
   3. In an emergency, people <u>can do</u> extraordinary things, like lift a truck.

In the previous sentences, the modal *can*:

   a. expresses the ability to do something.
   b. makes a request.
   c. gives permission.
   d. communicates a possibility.

Answer [3]

---

[1] If you selected choice <u>b</u>, you are correct.
[2] If you selected choice <u>c</u>, you are correct.
[3] If you selected choice <u>a</u>, you are correct.

Read the following sentences to determine the meaning of the underlined modal.

1. <u>Can</u> Amanda <u>drive</u> your car?
2. <u>Can</u> I <u>ask</u> a few simple questions?

In these two sentences, the modal *can* is used to:

a. express the ability to do something.
b. ask for permission.
c. give permission.
d. communicate a past possibility.

Answer [4]

Read the following sentences to determine the meaning of the underlined modal.

1. <u>Can</u> Larissa have a glass of water?
2. <u>Can</u> Pablo lower the volume on his stereo?

In these two sentences, the modal *can* is used to:

a. communicate a habitual action.
b. give an order.
c. complain.
d. make a request.

Answer [5]

Read the following sentences to determine the meaning of the underlined modal.

1. Learning to read and write <u>can be</u> a great challenge for a learning disabled child.
2. Anyone <u>can learn</u> to ride a bike.

In these sentences, the modal *can* is used to:

a. express a possibility.
b. communicate an impossibility.
c. give permission.
d. express a future event.

Answer [6]

---

[4] If you selected choice <u>b</u>, you are correct.
[5] If you selected choice <u>d</u>, you are correct.
[6] If you selected choice <u>a</u>, you are correct.

Read the following sentences to determine the meaning of the underlined modal.

1. Your mother <u>can't be</u> 95 years old! She looks so young.
2. That answer <u>cannot be</u> correct!

In these sentences, the modal *can* is used to:

a. express a possibility.
b. communicate an impossibility.
c. provide a suggestion.
d. a and b.

Answer [7]

The modal *can* is used to:

- **express ability,**
- **ask permission,**
- **make a request, or**
- **express a possibility or impossibility.**

e.g. Miguel <u>can lift</u> two hundred pounds. (←Ability)

Can Angelina <u>stay</u> at my house tonight? (←Permission)

Can Arturo <u>give</u> us a ride to school? (←Request)

Alicia <u>can win</u> the race with ease. (←possibility)

This <u>can't be</u> the right telephone number. (←impossibility)

The Modal Could

Read the following sentences to determine the meaning of the underlined modal.

1. She <u>could sing</u> like a bird as a young woman.
2. Stefano <u>could run</u> a marathon twenty-five years ago.

In these sentences, the modal *could* is used to:

a. express a conditional statement.
b. make a request.
c. communicate a past ability.

---

[7] If you selected choice <u>b</u>, you are correct.

d. all of these

Answer [8]

Read the following sentences to determine the meaning of the underlined modal.

1. <u>Could Maria use</u> your telephone?
2. <u>Could Sued take</u> a psychology course next term?

In these two sentences, the modal *could* is used to:

a. ask for permission in the present or future.

b. ask permission for a past action.

c. ask a question.

d. express ability.

Answer [9]

Read the following sentences to determine the meaning of the underlined modal.

1. Anyone <u>could get</u> lost on the New York City subway system.
2. That highway <u>could flood</u> after a hurricane.

In these two sentences, the modal *could* is used to:

a. a present hypothetical or imaginary situation.

b. a past situation.

c. a present impossibility.

d. a and c.

Answer [10]

Avoiding Common Errors with Modals

Read the following sentence and determine the mistake that was made.

Many years ago, Sheva <u>could makes</u> delicious fudge. (←incorrect)

In the previous sentence, the writer:

a. used the third person singular (makes) instead of the simple form of the verb (make) after a modal.

b. a past participle (made) after a modal instead of the simple form of the verb.

---

[8] If you selected choice c, you are correct.
[9] If you selected choice a, you are correct.
[10] If you selected choice a, you are correct.

c. a present participle (making) after the modal.

d. none of these

Answer [11]

When the rule for using a modal is applied correctly, the sentence states:

Many years ago, Sheva could make delicious fudge. (←correct)

The modal *could* is used to:

- **express past ability,**

- **present or future permission, or**

- **state a present hypothetical (imaginary) possibility.**

e.g. Manuel <u>could eat</u> ten hot dogs back then. (←past ability)

<u>Could I marry</u> your daughter? (←present or future permission)

After a storm, the ocean <u>could cover</u> that tiny island. (←hypothetical situation)

A modal is never followed by a verb in the third person singular.

e.g. Arturo could asks Marco about his problem. (←incorrect)

Controlled Exercises

Read each sentence carefully, and circle the correct response. Be sure to reference the rules just learned for the use of the modals can and could before you respond.

1. Sana (can, could) speak English, Farsi and Urdu. Her sister (can, could) speak Arabic when she was little, but she has forgotten most of it now.

2. The snow storm predicted for Sunday (can, could) cover Northern California with up two thirty-six inches of snow.

3. Research shows that a young child (can, could) learn to speak a second language with minimal effort.

4. Emilio (can, could) sing and dance when he was a teenager. Today, he (can, could) barely carry a tune.

---

[11] If you selected choice a, you are correct.

122

5. (Can, Could) Marta ask a question now?

6. That course (can, could) be very difficult for a person with no mathematical background.

7. (Can, Could) Alfanso and Stefano borrow your car? Yes, they (can, could), if they had driver's licenses!

8. (Can, Could) I bring my eight children to your dinner party?

9. Alfredo (can, could) resolve your computer problems, if he lived near you.

10. You (can never, could never) write the way Lorena did.

Practice Writing

1. Write three sentences using the modal *can* to

- express an ability,
- ask permission, and
- make a request.

As demonstrated in the following examples, be certain to specify if *can* is intended to express an ability, permission or a request.

e.g. *I can run one mile in less than five minutes.* (←Ability)

Can I ask you to do me a favor? (←Request)

Can Antonia and Nicola come for dinner tonight? (←Permission)

2. Write three sentences using the modal *could* to:

- express a past ability,
- ask present or future permission, and
- state a present hypothetical (imaginary) possibility.

As demonstrated in the following examples, be certain to specify if *could* is intended to express past ability, present/future permission or a hypothetical/imaginary possibility.

e.g. *When Alberto was 20, he could play basketball very well.* (←Past Ability)

Could I borrow $10,000 from you? (←Present/Future Permission)

Maria Elena could never be so beautiful. (←hypothetical or imaginary possibility)

The Modals May and Might

Read the following sentences to determine the meaning of the underlined modal.

1. Sarina <u>may go</u> to the rest room during class, because she has a medical problem.

2. Minors <u>may not consume</u> alcoholic beverages; however adults <u>may drink</u> alcohol.

In these sentences, the modal *may* is used to:

a. give permission.

b. explain why an activity is allowed or permitted.

c. communicate a hypothetical or imaginary situation.

d. a and b

Answer [12]

Read the following sentences to determine the meaning the underlined modal.

1. The beach <u>may be closed</u> because of a dangerous rip tide.

2. My girlfriend <u>may be</u> offended by his remark.

In these sentences, the modal *may* is used to:

a. express a past ability.

b. predict a result.

c. communicate a possibility.

Answer [13]

Read the following sentences to determine the meaning of the underlined modal.

1. My husband <u>might retire</u> next year.

2. The students who are frequently absent <u>might fail</u> their history course.

In these sentences, the modal *might* is used to:

a. offer advice.

b. give permission.

c. express a possibility.

Answer [14]

---

[12] If you selected choice <u>d</u>, you are correct.
[13] If you selected choice <u>c</u>, you are correct.
[14] If you selected choice <u>c</u>, you are correct.

> **The modal _may_ is used to:**
>
> - **give permission or explain that an activity is allowed or permitted, and**
> - **communicate a possibility.**
>
> e.g. Marisol <u>may return</u> home after midnight. (←gives permission, or states that activity that is allowed)
>
> The schools <u>may not open</u> today because of the terrible ice storm. (←a possibility)
>
> **The modal _might_ is used to express a possibility.**
>
> Nadia <u>might change</u> jobs next year. (←a possibility)

Read the following sentences to determine the meaning of the underlined modal.

1. Pietro <u>should take</u> his mother to the doctor.
2. Frank <u>should be</u> ready by now.

In these sentences, the modal _should_ is used to:

a. express an obligation or expectation.

b. give a suggestion or counsel.

c. state the intention of the subject.

d. all of these

Answer [15]

Read the following sentences to determine the meaning of the underlined modal.

1. Martina <u>shouldn't smoke</u> cigarettes.
2. People with diabetes <u>shouldn't eat</u> cake and candy.

In these sentences, the modal _should_ is used to:

a. state a wish.

b. promise of volunteer assistance.

c. provide advice or suggestions.

Answer [16]

---

[15] If you selected choice <u>a</u>, you are correct.

[16] If you selected choice <u>c</u>, you are correct.

Avoiding Common Errors with Modals

Read the following sentence and determine the mistake that was made.

1. Sidique and Ali might paid for their mother's new television. (←incorrect)

In the previous sentence, the writer used:

    a. an infinitive (to pay) instead of the simple form of the verb after a modal.

    b. a past participle (paid) after a modal, instead of the simple form of the verb.

    c. a present participle (paying) after the modal.

    d. none of these

Answer [17]

If the rule for using a modal is applied correctly, the sentence would state:

Sidique and Ali might pay for their mother's new television. (←correct)

Read the next sentence, and determine the mistake that was made.

1. Miguel should to call his parents more often. (←incorrect)

In the previous sentence, the writer used:

    a. an infinitive (to call), instead of the simple form of the verb after a modal.

    b. a past participle (called) after a modal, instead of the simple form of the verb.

    c. the their person singular (calls) after the modal.

    d. none of these

Answer [18]

If the rule for using a modal is applied correctly, the sentence would state:

Sidique and Ali might pay for their mother's new television. (←correct)

---

[17] If you selected choice <u>b</u>, you are correct.
[18] If you selected choice <u>a</u>, you are correct.

126

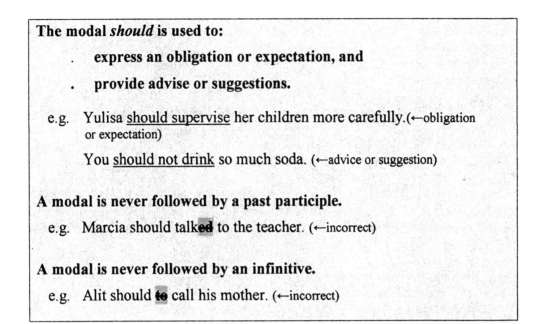

The modal *should* is used to:

- **express an obligation or expectation, and**

- **provide advise or suggestions.**

e.g. Yulisa <u>should supervise</u> her children more carefully.(←obligation or expectation)

You <u>should not drink</u> so much soda. (←advice or suggestion)

A modal is never followed by a past participle.

e.g. Marcia should talked to the teacher. (←incorrect)

A modal is never followed by an infinitive.

e.g. Alit should to call his mother. (←incorrect)

Controlled Exercises

Read each sentence carefully and circle the correct response. Be sure to reference the rules just learned about *may, might* and *should* before you respond.

1. Ariana and Lucia came home after 1 o'clock last night. They (may, might, should) not be permitted to stay out so late, for they are only twelve years old.

2. The children (may, might, should) leave the dinner table after they have eaten everything on their plates.

3. (May, Might, Should) I have a glass of cold water?

4. Francesca (may, might, should) learn to cook because eating take-out food is unhealthy and expensive.

5. Miguel (might, should) buy a new car next year if he gets a big bonus.

6. I'm not sure how Anna travels to work. She (should, might) commute on a bus because she doesn't like to take the subway to work.

7. Anna (should, might) take the train. It costs less than driving a car.

8. College students (may, might, should) attend every class and do all the assignments, if they want to pass.

9. Even though the students will object, the college (may, should) increase the tuition next year to pay for the increase in fuel.

10. College professors (may, might, should) be willing to help students when they have questions or academic problems. After all, isn't this why they have office hours?

Practice Writing

1. Write two sentences using the modal *may* to:

    - give permission or explain an activity is permitted, and
    - communicate a possibility.

Be certain to specify if *may* is intended to give permission or communicate a possibility.

e.g.   *You may sit down now.* (←give permission)

      The picnic may end early because of the rain. (←communicating a possibility)

2. Write one sentence using the modal *might* to express a possibility.

e.g.   *You might win the lottery someday.* (←a possibility)

3. Write two sentences using the modal *should* to:

    - express an obligation or expectation, and
    - provide advice or suggestions.

Be certain to specify if *should* is intended to express an obligation or expectation or to provide advice or suggestions.

e.g.   *You should help your grandmother when she shops for food.* (←expresses an obligation or expectation)

      Theodora should wear boots in the snow. (←provide advice or suggestions)

Error Analysis

Read each of the following sentences carefully. Then locate and correct any errors in the meaning and use of modals. If the sentence is written correctly, do not revise it.

1. The proposed tutoring center can foreign students obtain the individual assistance they require to complete their assignments.

2. When Asmita lived in India, she can not go to college because her family can not afford the tuition.

3. Lending money to relatives should create major family disagreements.

4. Even though many smokers want to quit, they continue to smoke because they may not afford an expensive smoke-enders program.

5. When parents always solve their children's problems, the children should never learns how to negotiate their problems.

6. Could you please lend me $10,000?

7. The Internet contains a tremendous amount of information, but it may not be accurate. Therefore, you may verify any data you obtain on-line.

8. Even though Carina's grandmother is seriously ill, she hasn't visited her. Clearly, Carina might visit her grandmother.

9. Clara might visits her parents on Sunday.

10. Parents may not pressure children to do well in school because excessive pressure can destroy a child's self-esteem.

The Modals Will and Would

Read the following sentences to determine the meaning of the underlined modal.

1. Mario <u>will return</u> from work late this evening.

2. My next class <u>will begin</u> at 4 o'clock.

In these sentences, the modal *will* is used to:

a. offer assistance.

b. make a prediction.

c. express a future action.

d. b and c

Answer [19]

Read the following sentences to determine the meaning of the underlined modal.

1. Marco <u>will fail</u> his physics course again.

2. Nicoletta <u>will never marry</u> Carlo.

In these sentences, the modal *will* is used to:

a. predict a past action.

b. predict a future action.

c. express a present action.

d. b and c

Answer [20]

Read the following sentences to determine the meaning of the underlined modal.

1. Patrizio <u>will drive</u> Graziella to the hospital.

2. HeeSoon <u>will draft</u> the budget report for you.

3. I <u>will help</u> you write the invitations.

In these sentences, the modal *will* is used to:

a. volunteer or promise to do something.

b. predict the future.

c. state one's intentions.

d. all of these.

Answer [21]

---

[19] If you selected choice <u>c</u>, you are correct.
[20] If you selected choice <u>b</u>, you are correct.
[21] If you selected choice <u>a</u>, you are correct.

> **The modal *will* is used to:**
>
> * **make a prediction or express a future action, and**
>
> * **volunteer or offer assistance.**
>
> e.g.   Yelena <u>will bake</u> the cake.(←volunteer or offer assistance)
>
> Pablo <u>will go</u> crazy when he sees the mess they made. (←make a prediction)

Read the following sentences to determine the meaning the underlined modal.

1. She <u>would walk</u> five miles everyday.

2. I <u>would wait</u> for his call every evening.

3. They <u>would come</u> to my house for Christmas dinner every year.

In these sentences, the modal *would* is used to:

a. state an untrue past fact.

b. express a characteristic or habitual past activity.

c. communicate a future event.

d. all of these

Answer [22]

> **The Modal *would* is used to express a characteristic or habitual past activity.**
>
> e.g.   Elvira <u>would invite</u> all her classmates to the party.(←characteristic or habitual past activity)

Controlled Exercises

Read each sentence carefully and circle the correct response. Be certain to reference the rules just learned about *will* or *would* before you respond.

1.   When I was a child, we (will, would) visit my grandparents on Sundays.

2.   Sidique (will, would) clean up the house after the party.

3.   I think that Ella (will, would) get angry when she hears the news.

---

[22] If you selected choice <u>b</u>, you are correct.

4.   Syed (will, would) get angry when he used to hear her unkind remarks.

5.   Pasquale (will, would) walk the dog and feed the cat when they are on vacation.

6.   Baljinder and Sudir are madly in love. Someday, they (will, would) marry each other.

7.   This year, it is the first time that my mother (will, would) prepare the holiday dinner for her family. Therefore, she (will, would) spend days shopping and cooking.

8.   In addition to what my mother is cooking, all of my aunts (will, would) prepare one special dish for the holiday.

9.   Before the holiday, the men (will, would) set tables up in our house so that everyone can sit comfortably while they eat.

10.   I remember how my grandmother (will, would) begin to prepare for the holiday two weeks before it arrived. She (will, would) be exhausted for days after this meal.

Practice Writing

1.   Write two sentences using the modal *will* to:

   * make a prediction about the future, and
   * volunteer assistance.

Be certain to specify if *will* is intended to express a prediction or to volunteer assistance.

e.g.   *You will be married and divorced in less than two years.* (←makes a prediction)

   Louisa and Paolo will baby-sit when you need help. (←volunteer assistance)

2.   Write a sentence using the modal *would* to:

- describe a characteristic or habitual past activity.

e.g. *Justin and Shifra would spend hours on the phone talking about how much they loved each other.* (←characteristic or habitual past activity.)

The Modal Must

Read the following sentences to determine the meaning of the underlined modal.

1. Marietta <u>must arrive</u> at work on time, or she will get fired.
2. Children <u>must attend</u> elementary school in the United States.
3. Noelle <u>must call</u> her parents every Sunday evening.

In these sentences, the modal *must* is used to:

a. offer a suggestion.

b. state a recommendation.

c. express an obligation.

d. a and b

Answer [23]

Read the following sentences to determine the meaning the underlined modal.

1. To stay healthy, children <u>must wear</u> a coat, a hat and gloves during the winter.
2. There <u>must be</u> a reason why so many students are absent.
3. She <u>must need</u> some help.

In these sentences, the modal *must* is used to express:

a. a necessity.

b. frustration.

c. an idea.

d. all of these

Answer [24]

---

[23] If you selected choice <u>c</u>, you are correct.
[24] If you selected choice <u>a</u>, you are correct.

> **The modal *must* is used to express:**
> - **an obligation, or**
> - **necessity.**
>
> e.g. Elvis <u>must eat</u> dinner before he can go out and play. (←obligation)
>
> Ana <u>must need</u> more cash by now. (←necessity)

Practice Writing

Write two sentences using the modal *must* to express:

- **an obligation, or**
- **a necessity.**

Be certain to specify if *must* expresses an obligation or a necessity.

e.g. *A minor child must obtain his/her parents written approval before getting married.* (←obligation)

 Elena must need a break by now. (←necessity)

The Modal Ought To

Read the following sentences to determine the meaning of the underlined modal.

1. Marietta <u>ought to save</u> some money, before she gets married.
2. A jury <u>ought to consider</u> all of the facts, before they make a decision.
3. People <u>ought to avoid</u> eating fried foods.

In these sentences, the modal *ought to* is used to:

a. give a recommendation or suggestion.
b. provide a command.
c. express an obligation.
d. a and b.

Answer [25]

---

[25] If you selected choice <u>a</u>, you are correct.

> **The modal *ought to* is used to express a suggestion.**
>
> e.g. You <u>ought to eat</u> your vegetables. (←suggestion)
>
> Pietro <u>ought to apply</u> for that job before someone else grabs it. (←suggestion)

Controlled Exercises

Read each sentence carefully and circle the correct response. Be sure to reference the rules just learned about *must* or *ought to* before you respond.

1. Children (must, ought to) brush their teeth after every meal to prevent cavities.

2. Clara is required to write two term papers for her history class. She (must, ought to) submit them by a specific date or she will receive a grade of F.

3. When college students don't understand a classroom lecture, they (must, ought to) ask the professor for assistance.

4. In my college, the students (must, ought to) attend 85 % of the classes if they want to pass the course.

5. When students (must, ought to) be absent from a class, they (must, ought to) inform their professors. Then, they (must, ought to) ask a classmate about any homework that was assigned.

6. Students (must, ought to) understand that they are responsible for their work in college and that a professor won't inform them if they don't complete the required assignments.

7. Maria (must, ought to) paint her bedroom pale blue.

8. When Carolina wants to stay out late, she (must, ought to) call her parents first to get their permission.

9.   Theresa (must, ought to) study more, if she wants to get straight As.

10.   I (must, ought to) buy a winter coat because it is extremely cold. I never owned a

      winter coat before this time because the weather in my homeland was much

      warmer.

Practice Writing

Write two sentences using the modal *ought to* to:

- express an obligation, and

- give a recommendation.

Be certain to specify if *ought to* is intended to express an obligation or a
recommendation.

e.g.   *Saria ought to write her composition, before she is too tired.* (←suggestion)

        The jury members ought to examine all the facts before they make a judgment.
        (←obligation)

Error Analysis

Read each of the following sentences carefully. Then locate and correct any errors in the
meaning and use of *all* the modals that you learned about in this chapter. However, if the
modals in the sentence are used correctly, do not revise them.

1.   The legalization of marijuana must prevented crime.

2.   In countries where the death penalty has been used, fewer violent crimes occur

      because citizens believe that they may abide by the law.

3.   According to the College's payment policy, all students should paid their tuition

      by a specific date, or the College would cancel their registration.

4.   When I was younger and expressed a desire to go to college, my parents can never

      understand why I wanted an education.

5. Mavish comes from a very traditional culture. A woman might cover her hair in public, and a marriage should not occur unless both sets of parents have given their blessing. This is a very important tradition.

6. In college, a student ought to take many required courses such as English composition.

7. Our college needs a bigger computer facility. Everyone always complains that they should wait more than an hour to gain access to a computer.

8. When college professors assign typed term papers, most students could word process them in the College's computer lab because they are too poor to purchase computers for their homes.

9. College students, who are caught cheating for the first time, would not be expelled. They ought to received a second chance.

10. Right now because our community is very urban and has no park or playground, the children may play on busy city streets, where they will be hit by a car or truck.

Practice in Context

Read the following story about lending money, and select the best modal that expresses the intended meaning.

Alicia's sister, Meera needed money. After years of unsuccessful treatments for infertility, Meera's insurance company (should, would, could) no longer pay for these services. Therefore, Meera and her husband (wouldn't, couldn't, shouldn't) afford to have a child. They feared their chance to be parents was disappearing, until Meera asked Alicia to lend her $20,000 for another procedure.

Alicia was reluctant to lend the money because they were trying to save money to purchase their first home, and they knew it (would, should) take years to accumulate that amount of money again. However, feeling pressured, they gave Meera the money anyway.

Money experts and family therapists believe it is risky when people lend money to relatives because money (will, can, should) be a curious subject. Although Alica (will, can, may) think she trusts Meera, she is entering into unknown territory because the new relationship is both psychological and financial.

Moreover, when you borrow money from a family member, they (will, can, may) want to know why you need it, and they (will, can, may) even criticize your need and believe it is frivolous. On the other hand, if a relative wants to borrow from you, you (would, might) find yourself questioning that person's choices and financial management, which (would, might) usually be none of your business.

If you still want to lend money, it is best to view the loan as a gift because if it isn't paid back, you (won't, can't, shouldn't) be angry. In fact, an unpaid loan (will, can) ruin what were once strong family relationships. Therefore, psychologists and financial managers suggest that you prepare not to get the money back because the relationship is worth more than the money.

Practice Writing

Write a composition explaining how you feel about lending relatives money. Be certain to explain how you would handle a situation if a relative refused to repay you.

The Passive Voice

Until now, you have written sentences using the active voice, which means that the subject of the sentence performs the action. In this chapter, you will learn the difference between the active and passive voice, so that you can form and use it correctly.

Read each set of sentences, and respond to the questions that follows.

1. a. Ann <u>writes</u> books.
    b. Books <u>are written</u> by Ann.

2. a. We <u>make</u> cakes for every party.
    b. Cakes <u>are made</u> ~~by us~~ for every party.

3. a. You <u>speak</u> Spanish.
    b. Spanish <u>is spoken</u> by you.

4. a. The cat <u>drinks</u> milk.
    b. Milk <u>is drunk</u> by the cat.

5. a. The women <u>clean</u> the house.
    b. The house <u>is cleaned</u> ~~by the women~~.

What tense does letter <u>a</u> in these examples use? _____ Answer [1]

What tense does letter <u>b</u> in these examples use?

   a. the past

   b. the present

   c. the present perfect

   d. none of these.

Answer [2]

If letters <u>a</u> and <u>b</u> are both in the present tense, why do the verbs use a different form? Their verb formats are different because:

   a. letter <u>a</u> is written in the active voice.

   b. letter <u>b</u> is written in the passive voice.

   c. the writer was confused

   d. a and b

Answer [3]

In letter <u>a</u> of these examples, who performs the action in each sentence?

   a. the adjective

   b. the object

---

[1] the present tense
[2] If you selected choice <u>b</u>, you are correct.
[3] If you selected choice <u>d</u>, you are correct.

c. the subject

d. the object of the preposition by.

Answer [4]

In letter b of these examples, who performs the action in each sentence?

    a. the subject

    b. the object

    c. the preposition

    d. the object of the preposition by.

Answer [5]

The difference between the active voice and the passive voice is that:

    a. in the active voice the subject performs the action.

    b. in the passive voice the subject of the sentence does not perform the action.

    c. in the passive voice you can indicate who performed an action by stating it as object of the preposition *by*.

    d. all of these.

Answer [6]

In the passive voice, is it necessary to state by whom an action is performed?

_____, in the passive voice, this information is optional.

Answer [7]

The difference in meaning between the active and passive voice is that:

    a. the passive voice does *not emphasize* who performed the action.

    b. in the passive voice, it is *not* always important to know who performed the action.

    c. the active voice stresses that the subject performed the action.

    d. all of these.

Answer [8]

---

[4] If you selected choice c, you are correct.

[5] If you selected choice d, you are correct.

[6] If you selected choice d you are correct.

[7] No

[8] If you selected choice d, you are correct.

Forming the Passive Voice

In English, if a verb is transitive, it means that the verb is:

   a. not followed by an adjective.

   b. followed by an object.

   c. not followed by an object.

   d. followed by an adjective.

Answer [9]

In contrast, an intransitive verb can:

   a. not be followed by an adjective.

   b. be followed by an object.

   c. not be followed by an object.

   d. not be followed by a prepositional phrase.

Answer [10]

Read the following sentence pairs to determine a rule for converting the active voice of a present tense verb to the passive voice.

↓subject ↓verb ↓object	↓subject ↓verb ↓object
a. Carlissa cooks dinner.	a. My husband and I play cards.
b. Dinner is cooked by Carlissa.	b. Cards are played by us.

object of active voice becomes subject in passive + _____ + **past participle** + **by** + **subject from active voice**

Answer[11]

Read the following sentences, and answer the question that follows them.

   a. This happens to me frequently.

   b. Every minute a person dies from heart disease.

---

[9] If you selected choice b, you are correct.

[10] If you selected choice c, you are correct.

[11] object of active voice becomes subject in passive + present tense of to be am, is, are + past participle + by + subject from active voice

141

These sentences cannot be made passive because:

   a. they don't have a subject.

   b. the verbs are intransitive and don't have an object.

   c. the verbs are transitive.

   d. all of these.

Answer [12]

The Active Voice versus the Passive Voice

When a transitive verb is followed by an object, it can be expressed in either the *active* or the *passive* voice, as in the following example.

    e.g. Nick plays the piano every evening.
          The piano is played by Nick every evening.

  • **In the active voice, the subject performs the action.**

    (Active Voice →) Michael repairs cars.

  • **In contrast, in the passive voice, the subject does not perform the action.**

    (Passive Voice →) Cars are repaired by Michael.

When a sentence is stated in the passive voice, you do *not* have to state who performed the action.

                  ↓**people who**
                  perform action
e.g. (Active Voice →) Ernest and Julio manufacture wine in California.

    (Passive Voice →) Wine is manufactured in California.

Read the following sentence and circle the objects.

   a. My sister buys me a gift.

   b. Her uncle gives the children money.

Answer [13]

---

[12] If you selected choice b, you are correct.
[13]   a.   My sister buys me a gift.
      b.   Her uncle gives the children money.

These sentences have _____ objects, which are called the direct and indirect objects.

Answer [14]

When a transitive verb has two objects, which object should be used as the subject in the passive voice sentence. You can use:

    a. either the direct or the indirect object.

    b. only the direct object

    c. only the indirect object.

    d. none of these.

Answer [15]

Direct and Indirect Objects

When a transitive verb has two objects, both objects can be used as the subject in the passive voice. The direct object usually refers to a thing or an object, while the indirect object refers to a person. Observe the following example.

                      indirect   direct
                      ↓object   ↓object

    e.g. Alana purchases Nancy a lottery ticket everyday.
           Nancy is purchased a lottery ticket everyday.
           A lottery ticket is purchased for Nancy everyday.

Controlled Practice

With a partner, convert each active voice present tense verb to the passive voice. However, if a verb is intransitive, do not make it passive.

e.g.   Louis studies art in college.

    Art is studied by Louis in college.

    Anita suffers from allergies.

    _____ (←This sentence cannot be expressed in the passive voice because the verb is intransitive verb and cannot take an object.)

---

[14]   two (The direct object usually refers to an object or thing while the indirect object refers to a person.)
[15] If you selected choice a, you are correct.

1. The police arrest criminals.

   _____

2. Those children play tag in the park.

   _____

3. Every nursing student receives training in CPR.

   _____

4. This problem occurs every day.

   _____

5. The teacher gives the students a test.

   _____

6. Ana Maria rarely makes a mistake.

   _____

7. We sing songs.

   _____

8. The women sing in the chorus.

   _____

9. That child consumes too much soda.

   _____

10. That dog barks all day long.

   _____

Practice Writing in the Passive Voice

In this exercise, you will be provided a list of nouns and verbs that are frequently used together. Select a noun and verb and write a sentence using present tense in the passive voice.

e.g.

Nouns	**Verbs**
breakfast, lunch, dinner	cook serve make prepare

Breakfast is served at 7 AM.

Dinner is prepared by a chef.

Lunch is served in the cafeteria.

	Nouns	**Verbs**
1.	gifts, a car, toys, clothes	purchase, give, buy, provide
2.	trophies, medals, prizes	award, present, grant
3.	books, novels, murder mysteries, biographies, letters	write, compose, create
4.	houses, buildings, bridges, parks	design, build, construct, develop, create
5.	tests, exams, homework, term papers	give, assign, do, copy, correct, edit, revise

The Passive Voice and the Past Tense

You have just learned how to convert active present tense sentences to the passive voice. Now you will learn how to form the passive voice in the past tense.

Read the following sentence pairs, and answer the questions that follow.

1. a. I <u>bought</u> a gift for Alba.
   b. A gift <u>was purchased</u> for Alba.

2. a. We <u>identified</u> the suspect.
   b. The suspect <u>was identified</u> by us.

3. a. You <u>found</u> a glove on the ground.
   b. A glove <u>was found</u> on the ground.

4. a. Sal <u>repaired</u> the car.   5. a. The doctors <u>examined</u> him.
   b. The car <u>was repaired</u>.   b. He <u>was examined</u> by the doctors.

What voice is used in letter a of these five sentence pairs? _____
Answer[16]

What voice is used in letter b of these five sentence pairs? _____
Answer[17]

What tense is used in letters a and b of these sentence pairs? _____
Answer[18]

You can distinguish between the active and the passive voice by:

    a. determining if the action was performed by the subject.

    b. determining in what tense the sentence is written.

    c. taking a wild guess.

    d. all of these.

Answer [19]

Can you complete the rule for forming the passive voice with the past tense?

object of the	_____		**(optional**
active voice +	_____	+ **past** +	**by + the**
becomes the	_____	**participle**	**subject of**
_____	_____	**verb**	**active voice)**

Answer[20]

---

[16] The active voice
[17] The passive voice
[18] The past tense
[19] If you selected choice <u>a</u>, you are correct.
[20]

object of the	past tense		(optional
active voice +	of verb	+ past +	by + the
becomes the	to be	participle	subject of
subject	was or were	verb	active voice)

> **The Past Tense in the Passive Voice**
>
> **The following form is used to make an active past tense verb passive.**
>
> e.g.   (Active Voice →) The men played cards.
>   (Passive Voice →) Cards *were played* by the men.

Controlled Practice

With a partner, convert each active voice past tense verb to the passive voice. However, if a verb is intransitive, do not make it passive. If it is not necessary to state by whom an action was performed, you can omit the prepositional phrase that begins with *by*.

e.g.   That restaurant served a wonderful meal.

   A wonderful meal was served.

1. A woman found a diamond ring on the bus.

    _____

2. The police apprehended the escaped prisoner.

    _____

3. The lifeguard swam across the pool.

    _____

4. The doctor performed many tests on my mother.

    _____

5. My professor contacted me at home.

    _____

6. Our class began at eight o'clock this morning.

    _____

7. After the party, the students cleaned the cafeteria.

   _____

8. The teacher provided the students many readings.

   _____

9. Someone destroyed the statue.

   _____

10. My team won the debate.

    _____

Practice in Context

Use the context to determine if you should use the present tense in active or passive voice.

Our willpower (test) _____ every day when we (decide)

_____ to stick to a diet or just to get out of bed to go to work. Through these

daily activities, we (push) _____ ourselves to determine what we (wish)

_____ to do.

The ability to resist temptation (describe) _____ as willpower or

self-control. For years, the concept of willpower has been examined by psychologists

who (desire) _____ to understand why some people (overindulge)

_____ in food, drugs, or alcohol. What scientists have determined is that

willpower (result) _____ from mental strength, which can be diminished

by physical and psychological forces.

Several investigations (indicate) _____ that self-control is a

limited resource, and it can be increased by the foods we eat. Laughter and memories can

also enhance a person's emotional strength. Moreover, one study (suggest)

_____ that we can improve our willpower through small practice activities because they (strengthen) _____ our coping mechanisms so that we can deal with greater challenges.

As any parent of a young child can tell you, learning self-control (produce) _____ a wide range of positive results. When children (engage) _____ in self-control, they (perform) _____ better in school, and success at work (facilitate) _____ by developing this skill, too. In fact, if we (observe) _____ most of the problems people (experience) _____, it can be predicted that self-control (involve) _____ in at some level.

Learning to control behavior (foster) _____ the development of character because it (permit) _____ people to obtain goals. However, because self-control (be) _____ a limited resource, it is best to make one realistic resolution and to stick to it because having several resolutions drains a person's emotional resources and undermine success.

Modals and the Passive Voice

What is a modal?

A modal is a word that:
   a. modifies a noun
   b. demonstrates an ability or willingness to do something
   c. modifies or describes a verb
   d. none of these

Answer [21]

---

[21] If you selected choice <u>b</u>, you are correct.

From the following lists, select the one that contains *modals*.

   a. to be, to have, to go, to do

   b. can, could, will, would, may, might, should, must

   c. a, an, the

   d. everyone, someone, everybody, anybody, etc.

Answer [22]

When modals, such as *can*, *must* or *would*, are used, what must follow them?

   a. a noun

   b. an adverb

   c. a verb in the simple form

   d. a past participle

Answer [23]

Observe the following examples that use modals in the passive voice.

1. a. I <u>can learn</u> that vocabulary.   2. a. We <u>must identify</u> the suspect.
     b. That vocabulary <u>can be learned</u>.   b. The suspect <u>must be identified</u>.

3. a. You <u>will receive</u> a gift.
     b. A gift <u>will be received</u>.

4. a. Rina <u>should make</u> a call.   5. a. He <u>should investigate</u> the problem.
     b. A call <u>should be made</u> by Rina.   b. The problem <u>should be investigated</u>.

Can you complete the rule for forming the passive voice with modals.

object of the active voice becomes the subject	+ _____	+ _____	+ past participle verb	+	(optional by + the subject of active voice)

Answer[24]

---

[22] If you selected choice <u>b</u>, you are correct.
[23] If you selected choice <u>c</u>, you are correct.

[24]

object of the active voice becomes the subject	modal can, could, will would, should, must, may, or might	+ be +	past participle verb	+	(optional by + the subject of active voice)

Can you write a sentence using a modal in the passive voice?

e.g. *A letter of recommendation can be written by any professor.*

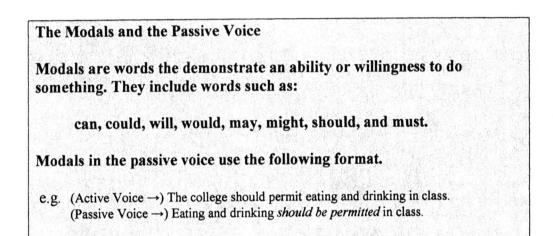

The Modals and the Passive Voice

Modals are words the demonstrate an ability or willingness to do something. They include words such as:

can, could, will, would, may, might, should, and must.

Modals in the passive voice use the following format.

e.g. (Active Voice →) The college should permit eating and drinking in class.
(Passive Voice →) Eating and drinking *should be permitted* in class.

Controlled Practice

With a partner, convert each of the underlined verbs and modals to the passive voice, if the verb is transitive. If it is not necessary to state by whom the action was performed, you can omit the *by* prepositional phrase.

e.g.   American citizens <u>will elect</u> a new president.

*A new president **will be elected** by the American citizens.*

1. Every child <u>can receive</u> a free education in the United States.

    _____

2. College students <u>should attend</u> all their classes.

    _____

3. Teachers <u>must explain</u> new material carefully.

    _____

4. You <u>will write</u> a ten-page term paper.

    _____

5. His mother <u>should permit</u> him to drive the new car.

   _____

6. The police <u>might question</u> Paolo today.

   _____

7. Tomas <u>would not lie</u> to me.

   _____

8. Ignazia and Franco <u>could build</u> a big house on that land.

   _____

9. We <u>must clean</u> our rooms.

   _____

10. Sadaf and Ahmed <u>might write</u> a book.

    _____

Error Analysis

The following sentences all contain errors in the use modals in the active and passive voice. Read each sentence carefully to locate and correct any mistakes.

1. Children should understood that their emotions will be easier to manage when they learn self-control.

2. Emotional outbursts could be destroyed a person's opportunity for job advancement.

3. The whole world could be affect by one person's poor decision.

4. An open wound must been cleaned thoroughly, and then it should cover with a sterile bandage to prevent infection.

5. Smoking should be prohibit in all public buildings because passive smoking can cause cancer.

6. People, especially teens, should not allowed to play loud music in public places because this noise annoys other people.

7. In the United States, many people put their older relatives in nursing homes, but in my homeland, elderly parents must take care of by their children.

8. If Marisa gets that promotion, she might be providing a company car and an expense account.

9. The cultural festival should be occurred next week after classes end.

10. The college should be expelled students for cheating.

Practice in Context

Many newspaper articles use the passive voice when writing about crimes because the reporters want to emphasize the criminal act, not the people who arrested or convicted the criminal. With this in mind, read the following article, and wherever possible convert the underlined verbs to the passive voice. However, if a verb is intransitive, do not make it passive. In addition, if it is *not* necessary to state by whom the action was performed, omit the prepositional phrase that begins with *by*. Since several different tenses and modals are used in this exercise, be certain to use the correct passive tense format.

On December 1st, the police caught Mickey Stevens exiting the back door of a private residence. When the police questioned Stevens about his suspicious behavior, he claimed, "This is my girlfriend's house. She gave me a key to let myself in when she wasn't home." However, when the police examined the contents of his pockets, they found jewelry, cash, an ATM card and a woman's driver's license. To verify Steven's story, the police contacted the owner of the house, but she indicated that she didn't know Stevens. Consequently, the police arrested Stevens, and they charged him with robbery.

The next day, the district attorney arraigned Stevens for breaking and entering, and the judge set bail at $50,000. Since Stevens could not pay the bail, the judge remanded him to jail until the trial. Several months later at the trial, a jury found Stevens guilty, and the judge sentenced him to two years in prison.

If Stevens stays out of trouble, prison officials might release him early for good behavior. While on parole, Stevens must check in with his parole officer, and he cannot consume alcohol or carry a firearm. If he violates the conditions of his parole, the police will incarcerate him again.

The Passive Voice with Other Tenses

Until now, we have only discussed the use of the passive voice in the present tense, past tense and with modals. However, since the passive voice can be used in any tense with a transitive verb, the following charts will specify the rules that are applied when other tenses are formed in the passive voice.

Present Progressive Tense

Observe how the present progressive is formed in the passive voice.

Active Voice	Passive Voice
I am baking a pie.	A pie is being baked.
You are telling many conflicting stories.	Many conflicting stories are being told.
The man is wearing a raincoat.	A raincoat is being worn by the man.
She is writing a book about the murder.	A book is being written about the murder.
The cat is chasing a mouse.	A mouse is being chased by the cat.
We are speaking French.	French is being spoken.
They are purchasing tickets.	Tickets are being purchased.

Can you write the rule for forming the passive voice in the present progressive tense?

object of the active voice becomes the _____	+ _____	+ _____	+ past participle verb	+ (optional by + the subject of active voice)

Answer [25]

---

[25] object of the active voice becomes the subject + present tense to be (am is, are) + present participle to be (being) + past participle + (optional by the subject of verb active voice)

154

Can you write a sentence using the present progressive tense in the passive voice?

e.g.   *The papers are being marked by the teachers now.*

Past Progressive Tense

Observe how the past progressive tense is formed in the passive voice.

Active Voice	Passive Voice
I <u>was serving</u> lunch.	Lunch <u>was being served</u>.
You <u>were asking</u> too many questions.	Too many questions <u>were being asked</u>.
He <u>was discussing</u> a problem.	A problem <u>was being discussed</u>.
She <u>was making</u> a suggestion.	A suggestion <u>was being made</u>.
The rabbit <u>was eating</u> a carrot.	A carrot <u>was being eaten</u> by the rabbit.
We <u>were discussing</u> the article.	The article <u>was being discussed</u>.
They <u>were purchasing</u> stamps.	Stamps <u>were being purchased</u>.

Can you complete the rule for forming the passive voice in the past progressive tense?

object of the active voice becomes the subject	+	past tense of to be (was/were)	+	_____ _____	+	_____ _____	+	(optional by + the subject of active voice)

Answer [26]

Can you write a sentence using the past progressive tense in the passive voice?

e.g.   *I was being criticized for my mistake.*

---

[26] object of the active voice becomes the subject + past tense to be (was, were) + present participle to be (being) + past participle + (optional by the subject of verb active voice)

155

> **Using the Passive Voice in the Progressive Tenses**
>
> **The Present Progressive Tense in the Passive Voice**
>
> **The following format is used to convert an active present progressive verb to the passive.**
>
> **e.g.** (Active Voice →) The college is closing the bookstore.
> (Passive Voice →)The bookstore *is being closed.*
>
> **The Past Progressive Tense in the Passive Voice**
>
> **The following format is used to convert an active past progressive verb to the passive voice.**
>
> **e.g.** (Active Voice →) The woman *was cleaning* the house.
> (Passive Voice →)The house *was being cleaned* by the woman.

Controlled Practice

With a partner, convert each of the underlined progressive tense verbs to the passive voice, if the verb is transitive. You can omit the prepositional *by* phrase, if it is not necessary to state by whom the action was performed. Please note that both the present and past progressive tenses are included in this exercise.

e.g.   My company is interviewing new employees.

New employees are being interviewed by my company.

1. Everyone was watching the news broadcast.

   _____

2. Our student government is holding a cultural festival.

   _____

3. The professors are marking our final exams.

   _____

4. The child was watching a baseball game.

   _____

5. I am preparing for a trip to South America.

   _____

6. The two politicians <u>were discussing</u> several controversial issues.

_____

7. Antonio and Teresa <u>are eating</u> dinner.

_____

8. Elena <u>is washing</u> the dishes.

_____

9. You <u>were reading</u> a book.

_____

10. Alfredo <u>was taking</u> notes during class.

_____

Present Perfect Tense

Observe how the present perfect tense is formed in the passive voice.

Active Voice	Passive Voice
I <u>have written</u> the term paper.	The term paper <u>has been written</u>.
You <u>have wasted</u> valuable time.	Valuable time <u>has been wasted</u>.
He <u>has rented</u> a car.	A car <u>has been rented</u>.
She <u>has drafted</u> a letter.	A letter <u>has been drafted</u>.
Jealousy <u>has created</u> many problems.	Many problems <u>have been created</u> by jealousy.
We <u>have contacted</u> her.	She <u>has been contacted.</u>
My teammates <u>have lost</u> many games.	Many games <u>have been lost</u>.

Can you complete the rule for forming the passive voice in the present perfect tense?

object of the active voice becomes the subject	+	present tense of to have _____	+	_____	+	past participle verb	+	(optional by + the subject of active voice)

Answer [27]

Can you write a sentence using a modal in the passive voice?

e.g.   *Every piece of candy has been eaten.*

_____

Past Perfect Tense

Observe how the past perfect tense is formed in the passive voice.

Active Voice	Passive Voice
I <u>had contacted</u> her previously.	She <u>had been contacted</u> previously.
You <u>had learned</u> an important lesson by that time.	An important lesson <u>had been learned</u> by that time.
He <u>had neglected</u> his health.	His health <u>had been neglected</u>.
She <u>had sung</u> that song.	That song <u>had been sung</u> by her.
His dissatisfaction <u>had caused</u> conflicts.	Conflicts <u>had been caused</u> by his dissatisfaction.
We <u>had informed</u> her of the problem.	She <u>has been informed</u> of the problem.
Those students <u>had failed</u> several courses that semester.	Several courses <u>had been failed</u> by those students that semester.

---

[27] object of the active voice becomes the subject + present tense of have (has, have) + past participle to be (been) + past participle of verb + (optional by the subject of verb active voice)

Can you complete the rule for forming the passive voice in the past perfect tense?

| object of the active voice becomes the subject | + | past tense of to have (had) | + | _____ | + | _____ _____ | + | (optional by + the subject of active voice) |

Answer [28]

Can you write a sentence using a modal in the passive voice?

e.g.   *Marissa had been taught to drive previously.*

_____

> **The Passive Voice and the Perfect Tenses**
>
> **The Present Perfect Tense in the Passive Voice**
>
> **The following format is used to convert an active present perfect tense verb to the passive voice.**
>
> **e.g.** (Active Voice →) The men *have purchased* the boat.
> (Passive Voice →)The boat *has been purchased* by the men.
>
> **The Past Perfect Tense in the Passive Voice**
>
> **The following format is used to convert an active past perfect tense verb to the passive voice.**
>
> **e.g.** (Active Voice →) The child *had eaten* an apple.
> (Passive Voice →) An apple *had been eaten* by the child.

---

[28] object of the active voice becomes the subject + past tense of have (had) + past participle to be (been) + past participle of verb + (optional by the subject of verb active voice)

159

Controlled Practice

With a partner, convert each of the underlined perfect tense verbs to the passive voice, if the verb is transitive. Please note that both the present perfect and past perfect tenses are included in this exercise. You can omit the prepositional phrase *by*, if it is not necessary to state by whom the action was performed.

e.g.   Ashima <u>had purchased</u> a second hand car before that time.

*A second hand car **had been purchased** by Ashima before that time.*

1. They <u>had ignored</u> her complaints.

   _____

2. Frank and Mary <u>have gone</u> for a walk.

   _____

3. Rina and I <u>have studied</u> Italian for years.

   _____

4. My daughter <u>had played</u> soccer years ago.

   _____

5. They <u>have lost</u> the receipt for the computer.

   _____

6. The honey <u>had sweetened</u> my tea.

   _____

7. Her medical knowledge <u>has helped</u> many ill people.

   _____

8. They <u>had considered</u> many different alternatives.

   _____

9. You <u>have asked</u> her for an excuse before.

   _____

10. Maurizio and Paolo <u>had learned</u> three languages by that time.

   _____

Practice in Context

Read each of the following paragraphs and re-write them converting the underlined active verbs to the passive voice. Be certain to determine in which tense each verb is written before converting it so that the meaning of the sentence is not altered. Whenever possible, omit the prepositional *by* phrase.

1. Recently <u>released</u> a study about the health of people in the suburbs. They <u>revealed</u> some interesting findings, after they <u>evaluated</u> data from nearly 8,600 people. In their analyses, they discovered that suburbanites <u>had reported</u> more health problems such as headaches, breathing problems, and high blood pressure. They concluded that people who live in dense urban areas get more exercise than people who live in suburban areas because suburbanites typically drive to their destinations. In contrast, city dwellers reported walking to stores, buses, schools several times each day. One woman who had migrated to the suburbs stated that after she had moved out of the city, she stopped walking and instead started driving. She <u>could not reach</u> her destination by foot anymore. These results were quite unanticipated. The researchers <u>expected</u> an entirely different outcome. They had assumed that living in the suburbs around trees, flowers would be healthier. However, since some critics <u>are questioning</u> their conclusions, other researchers <u>will reexamine</u> these findings.

2. Heart disease is no longer the number one killer of Americans. Instead, cancer deaths <u>have surpassed</u> heart disease. The primary reason for the decline in cardiac deaths has resulted from the reduction in cigarette smoking. Smoking is the lead cause of sudden cardiac deaths; and, after two or three years, quitting smoking nearly <u>eliminates</u> this risk. However, giving up smoking doesn't have the same impact on cancer. Smoking

can damage cells in many organs of the body, and this damage is irreversible and may take decades to appear. Another reason why the reduction in cardiac deaths has occurred is because of more advanced treatments of high blood pressure and cholesterol. In addition, because of better dietary and health education, Americans have reduced their intake of fatty foods. Finally, bypass surgery and angioplasty have reduced the number of heart attacks. However, very few comparable measures can protect against cancer. While people are advised to exercise regularly, maintain a normal weight, limit meat intake and eat plenty of fruits and vegetables, this approach may require a lifetime of effort to be successful.

Error Analysis

The following sentences all contain errors in the use modals in the active and passive voice. Read each sentence carefully to locate and correct any mistakes.

1. Self-motivated children become more independent and try to do their best to reach their goals. Therefore, these children are succeeded in life.

2. My job is not stable, and my salary is varied.

3. Web pages cannot be open because my computer is broken.

4. Our neighborhood is very urban so that most people are force to exercise on busy streets and sidewalks.

5. Students will be discouraging from continuing their educations if the college is increased the tuition again.

6. Many people believe that violent murderers should be execute, but I am disagreed because I don't think anyone has the right to take another person's life.

7. If our city constructs a mall, our residents will been offer more job opportunities.

8.   Drug abuse is happened in many foreign countries today.

9.   The College's computer facility rarely used for academic purposes by students.

10.   A large donation has given to the college by an anonymous donor.

11.   The criminal paroled after completing a few years in jail.

12.   In the United States, most parents are always at work, so that their children are never learn to respect adults.

13.   This type of car accident has been occurred many times at that corner.

14.   After a camera had installed on that corner, the number of accidents reduced.

15.   The employees weren't permit to speak to the media.

Practice Writing

Write a composition about one of the following topics.

1.   In the United States, many people believe the death penalty is the only way to prevent violent criminals from hurting innocent people while others think that killing a criminal is immoral and inhumane. Write a composition explaining why you agree or disagree with the death penalty. Underline or highlight every sentence where the passive voice is used.

2.   In many major cities, the police are installing video surveillance cameras on busy urban streets to monitor traffic violations and to prevent crimes. However, many people believe that videotaping pedestrians is an invasion of their privacy. Write a composition explaining why you agree or disagree with the use of video surveillance cameras on busy urban streets. Underline or highlight every sentence where the passive voice is used.

Independent Clauses

The goal of this unit is to teach you to:

- understand what an independent clause is;
- connect independent clauses correctly; and
- avoid run on sentences and comma splices.

Independent Clauses

An independent clause is:

a. a prepositional phrase

b. a complete sentence

c. an adjective clause

d. an adverbial clause

Answer [1]

Independent clauses are also called:

a. main clauses

b. conditional clauses

c. adjective clauses

d. adverbial clauses

Answer [2]

Which of the following statements are independent clauses?

a. We had coffee and muffins for breakfast.

b. If I am late for class

c. Every time she calls me

d. My friends come from different countries.

e. Because she is young and beautiful

f. choices a and d

Answer [3]

---

[1] If you selected choice <u>b</u>, you are correct.
[2] If you selected choice <u>a</u>, you are correct.
[3] If you selected choice <u>f</u>, you are correct.

> **Independent Clauses**
>
> An independent clause is a *complete sentence* that makes sense by itself, and it is also referred to as a **main clause**.
>
> e.g. I speak three languages.
> You took a psychology course last year.
> Maria wants to take piano lessons.
> We practice writing every day.
> Ahmed and Sadaf came from the same country.

In English, one main clause contains one sentence or one complete thought, as in the following examples.

Emilio drives to work every day.

Renata loves pizza.

You can sing beautifully.

Frank doesn't drink coffee.

When a sentence contains two main clauses, it is called a:

a. simple sentence.

b. fragment.

c. compound sentence.

d. none of these.

Answer [4]

A compound sentence can contain *no more than* _____ main clauses.

a. one

b. two

c. three

d. four

Answer [5]

---

[4] If you selected choice c, you are correct.
[5] If you selected choice b, you are correct.

165

In English, a sentence should not contain more than two main clauses. Read the following sentences:

- underline the main clauses;
- determine how many main clauses each sentence contains; and
- specify word used to connect the main clauses.

	number of main clauses	word used to connect main clauses	
a.	2	and	<u>Anna will bake the cake</u>, and <u>I will buy the candles</u>.
b.			Eva loves to sing, so she joined the college chorus.
c.			Sean enjoys his English class, but he doesn't pay attention in Chemistry.
d.			David must pass the written driver's exam, or he can not take driving lessons.
e.			The student immediately raised her hand, yet she didn't know the answer.
f.			The audience applauded, for the opera had been wonderful.
g.			Lisa won't call Carina, nor will she e-mail her.

Each sentence contains _____ main clauses. Answer [6]

In each sentence, the two main clauses are separated by:

   a. a conjunction

   b. a comma

   c. a comma followed by a conjunction

   d. a period.

Answer [7]

---

[6] two

[7] If you selected choice c, you are correct.

Which list contains coordinating conjunctions?

   a. although, because, if, when, before, after, until

   b. and, but, so, yet, or, nor, for

   c. however, furthermore, additionally, moreover

   d. a and b

Answer [8]

In English, two sentences *cannot* be separated by a _____.

   a. comma

   b. comma and a conjunction

   c. period

   d. question mark

Answer [9]

When two independent clauses are separated by a comma, this mistake is called a

_____ Answer [10]

Connecting Independent or Main Clauses

In English, a compound sentence can contain *only two independent clauses*.
When a sentence contains *two main clauses*, they are connected as follows.

e.g.   I love to watch old movies, ***but*** my daughter prefers action films.
       Alica visits a foreign country every year, ***and*** I usually travel with her.

Two sentences cannot be separated by a comma. If they are, you have
created a ***comma splice,*** as in the following example.

↓ comma splice
(incorrect →) I was frightened, I didn't know what to do.

(correct →)   I was frightened, **and** I didn't know what to do.

---

[8] If you selected choice <u>b</u>, you are correct.
[9] If you selected choice <u>a</u>, you are correct.
[10] comma splice

Controlled Practice

With a partner, combine the following sentences using the rules just learned. Be certain to use a conjunction that conveys the correct meaning.

e.g.   Louisa went to her Chemistry class. The instructor was absent.

Louisa went to her Chemistry class, but the professor was absent.

1. Ludmila has twin boys. They are ten years old.

    _____

2. Baljinder baked a birthday cake. She wrote "Happy Birthday" on it.

    _____

3. The children in our area want to play baseball. Our neighborhood doesn't have

    baseball field.

    _____

4. Melissa doesn't like mathematics. She won't take a calculus course.

    _____

5. Our guests can stay at my house. They can also stay at a local hotel.

    _____

6. The students purchased the required composition textbook. It cost $500.

    _____

7. My computer was broken. I used one in the library.

    _____

8. I love living in New York. I am afraid to go out alone late at night.

    _____

9. The women cleaned the house. They also cooked a big meal for us.

    _____

10. We can drive to work. We can take mass transit, too.

Practice Writing

With a partner, write three compound sentences that contain two main clauses about your family, your country or homeland. Be certain to connect the main clauses using the rules just learned.

e.g.   *I moved to this country twenty years ago, but my family still lives in Korea.*

1. _____

    _____

2. _____

    _____

3. _____

    _____

Each of the following statements is connected incorrectly. After you read them and locate the error, answer the questions that follow.

   a. Babies laugh children cry.

   b. My parents encouraged me to get an education they didn't pressure me.

   c. Competition doesn't improve friendships it can destroy them.

Each of the above sentences contains _____ main clauses. Answer [11]

What is done incorrectly in each of these sentences?

   a. Two sentences are pushed together without the correct punctuation.

   b. The writer created run-on sentences.

   c. Each of these examples contains two main clauses, but they aren't connected correctly.

   d. all of these

Answer [12]

---

[11] two

[12] If you selected choice d, you are correct.

169

Run-on sentences occur when a writer pushes two sentences together without using the correct punctuation.

Which of these sentences are punctuated correctly?

    a. Babies laugh. Adults cry.

    b. Babies laugh, but adults cry.

    c. My parents encouraged me to get an education. They didn't pressure me

    d. My parents encouraged me to get an education, but they didn't pressure me.

    e. Competition doesn't improve friendships, but it can destroy them.

    f. Competition doesn't improve friendships. It can destroy them.

    g. all of these

Answer [13]

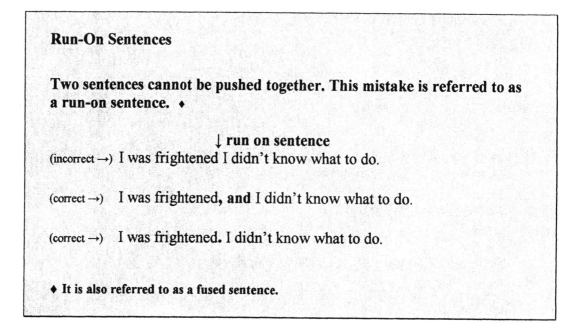

Run-On Sentences

Two sentences cannot be pushed together. This mistake is referred to as a run-on sentence. ♦

                    ↓ run on sentence

(incorrect →) I was frightened I didn't know what to do.

(correct →)   I was frightened, **and** I didn't know what to do.

(correct →)   I was frightened. I didn't know what to do.

♦ **It is also referred to as a fused sentence.**

Error Analysis

Read each of the following sentences, and correct any comma splices or run-on sentences.

     A recent study has reported that people who suffer from moderate depression can reduce their symptoms by exercising regularly. For years, exercise has been considered a mood enhancer, many physically disabled people have claimed to feel better emotionally

---

[13] If you selected choice g, you are correct.

when they exercise. Therefore, a group of researchers examined the question of whether or not exercise can reduce the symptoms of depression.

The participants in the study were adults, they all suffered from depression. They were divided into different groups, each group participated in different types of exercise. Some subjects used a treadmill others walked and some exercised on a stationary bike. Only one person performed flexibility exercises.

After approximately three months into the exercise program, the researchers discovered that exercise reduced depression, the participants who worked out for thirty minutes at least three times a week reported half as many symptoms of depression. This study suggests that the more these subjects exercised the less depressed they felt, but insufficient aerobic activity resulted in more complaints of depression.

It should be noted that the participants exercised with a partner or in a group so the social interaction may have contributed to the reduction in depression, too. The most important finding is that the benefits the subjects received were comparable to those achieved with medication and counseling. To verify these results, it is suggested this study be repeated with a larger population some of the participants should exercise in groups, others should work out in pairs or alone, this will allow researchers to determine if the beneficial outcomes resulted from the exercise routine or the social interaction. This follow-up study will verify what truly reduces the depression.

Reducing Main Clauses

Examine each of the following sentence pairs, and answer the questions below them.

1. a. I studied for the test, but I didn't get a good grade.

   b. I studied for the test, but didn't get a good grade.

2. a. You were absent seven times, and you didn't submit ten assignments.

   b. You were absent seven times, and didn't submit ten assignments.

3. a. Lara completed her degree, and she has been hired by a bank.

   b. Lara completed her degree, and has been hired by a bank.

Answer the following questions about these three pairs of sentences.

Letter <u>a</u> of each sentence pair contains _____ main clauses. Answer [14]

Letter <u>b</u> of each sentence pair contains _____ main clause(s). Answer [15]

In letter <u>b</u>, the writer has _____ the second main clause.

   a. omitted

   b. reduced

   c. forgotten

   d. added

Answer [16]

When a compound sentence has *two* main clauses and the subject in both main clauses is the same, you can:

   a. eliminate the second main clause.

   b. reduce the second main clause by omitting the subject.

   c. add a third main clause.

   d. none of these

Answer [17]

---

[14] two

[15] one

[16] If you selected choice <u>b</u>, you are correct.

[17] If you selected choice <u>b</u>, you are correct.

Read the following sentence pairs, and observe how they have been reduced.

1. a. The students were reading. They were studying, and they were writing.

    b. The students were reading, studying and writing.

2. a. Anita should have attended class. She should have completed her assignments, and she should have studied more.

    b. Anita should have attended class, completed her assignments, and studied more.

Letter <u>a</u> of each pair of sentences contains _____ main clauses. Answer [18]

Letter <u>b</u> of each pair of sentences contains _____ main clauses. Answer [19]

According to these examples, when there are *three* main clauses, the second and third clauses can be reduced if:

   a. the subject is different in each clause.

   b. the subject is plural in each clause.

   c. the subject is the same in each clause.

   d. none of these

Answer [20]

You can also eliminate the auxiliary verb in the second and third main clauses, if:

   a. the subject is the same in each clause.

   b. the subject and the auxiliary verb are the same in each clause.

   c. the subject is the same, but the auxiliary verb is different in each clause.

   d. none of these

Answer [21]

Read the following sentence.

   I had eaten, but my son had not eaten yet.

   My sister was singing, and I was dancing.

---

[18] three

[19] one

[20] If you selected choice <u>c</u>, you are correct

[21] If you selected choice <u>b</u>, you are correct.

The second clause cannot be reduced because:

a. the subjects in two main clauses are different.

b. the auxiliary verbs are different in the first and second main clauses.

c. the two main clauses are unrelated.

d. all of these

Answer [22]

Controlled Practice

In the following exercise, reduce the second and third main clauses, if permissible.

e.g.   I had cleaned the house, and I had cooked a meal.

   I had cleaned the house, and cooked a meal.

1. He had eaten every snack, and he had drunk all the soda.

   _____

2. Carla went to work on Monday, but she left early.

   _____

3. Ahmed will live at home. He will attend college, and he will work part time.

   _____

4. Alicia and I purchased two I-Pods, and we gave them to my parents as gifts.

   _____

5. Our professor is very strict. I like him, but some students dislike him.

   _____

6. My parents lived in China most of their lives, but they moved to New York last year.

   _____

7. The house was filthy, and it hadn't been painted in years.

   _____

---

[22] If you selected choice <u>a</u>, you are correct.

8. The college will host a cultural festival, and the students and faculty will participate.

_____

9. Sana studies very hard, and she receives high honors each semester.

_____

10. You must attend every class, and you must do all of your assignments carefully.

_____

Error Analysis

Read the following composition and make any necessary corrections to connect the main clauses correctly. Be certain to search for comma splices, run-on sentences, and mistakes in reduced main clauses. When possible, reduce a main clause to make this composition concise (brief and to the point).

Recent studies have revealed that some people absolutely love their jobs, they aren't just happy to be employed, but they love what they do. These people jump out of bed with enthusiasm every morning because they want to go to work, these folks claim they would continue to work even if they won the lottery.

Who are these insane people who love to work? One woman left a high paying, pressure-cooker job in banking, and she now owns a nail salon. She earns less than half of what she used to make but she claims her clients are pleased with her services, no one screams at her or threatens to get her fired. She doesn't dread seeing her customers, but looks forward to their visits to her salon.

These happily employed people appear to have one thing in common they have jobs that allow them to be creative, and they are appreciated, their clients are friends, almost like members of their families. One man detested the frantic, fast pace that he maintained in an advertising firm. Today he is self-employed as a chef in a restaurant.

To find this level of job satisfaction, people may think that they have to select unusual careers or give up high incomes, but that is not true, many people in traditional jobs claim to enjoy their work, too. Contentment in traditional areas of employment seems to occur when co-workers admire and respect each other. They feel like part of a greater team effort. In fact, many professionals such as teachers and bankers report high levels of job satisfaction, they live for their jobs and dread the prospect of retirement.

This study produced some surprising results in a world filled with employees who count the days until retirement, and it suggests that many employees reap pleasure and satisfaction from their jobs when they have good co-workers and satisfied customers.

Practice Writing

Write a composition explaining the reasons:

- why a person would take a less prestigious, or lower paying job that they like, or
- why you think a person would continue to work at a job they dislike, or
- why a person should quit a job that he/she strongly hates.

Be certain to connect your main and reduced clauses correctly.

Conjunctive Adverbs and the Semi-Colon

Earlier in this chapter, you learned that two main clauses can be connected by placing a comma and a conjunction after the first main clause, and before the second main clause. However, in more formal writing, it is sometimes necessary to use a conjunctive adverb and a semi-colon. Therefore, this section will instruct you in their use.

Select the list that contains conjunctive adverbs.

- a. and, but, so, yet, or, nor, for
- b. because, although, even though, before, after
- c. furthermore, moreover, additionally, therefore, however

d. b and c

Observe the following sentences that are punctuated correctly.

a. The student missed ten classes; therefore, he failed his history course.

b. The woman witnessed the murder; however, she would not testify in court.

c. The judge fined the girl; in addition, he ordered her to perform community service for six months.

Write the rule for using conjunctive adverbs to connect two main clauses.

     first   second
main clause + _____ + _____ + _____ + main clause   answer [24]

Observe what occurs in the following examples when a conjunctive adverb begins a sentence.

a. The student missed ten classes, so his teacher failed him. Therefore, the student must repeat the course.

b. The woman witnessed the murder, but she would not testify in court. Consequently, the criminal was not convicted.

c. The police officer and a witness testified that teenage girl ran a stop sign, so the judge found her guilty. Thus, the young woman had to pay a fine and perform community service for six months.

When the conjunctive adverb is the first word of a sentence, a _____ must follow it. Answer [25]

The writer did not connect these three clauses because:

a. a compound sentence can only contain two main clauses.

b. a semi-colon can only be used before a conjunctive adverb.

c. it would confuse the reader.

d. all of these

Answer [26]

---

[23] If you selected choice c, you are correct.
[24] first main clause + semi-colon + conjunctive adverb + comma + second main clause
[25] comma
[26] If you selected choice a, you are correct.

Warning:

Occasionally, you may be tempted to begin a sentence with the conjunctions *and* or *but*. However, in formal written English, it is better to avoid this practice. Instead, you can begin the sentence with a conjunctive adverb such as additionally, moreover, however, etc.

Using Conjunctive Adverbs to Connect Main Clauses

Conjunctive Adverbs include the following words:

additionally,	in addition,	furthermore,	moreover,	however,
nevertheless,	nonetheless,	besides,	indeed,	thus,
therefore,	consequently,	as a result,	in contrast,	hence

In formal writing, conjunctive adverbs can be used to connect two main clauses by using the following rule.

e.g.   The police arrested a suspect; **however,** he had an alibi.

The professor had explained the math problem clearly; **therefore,** the students understood it well.

Using Conjunctive Adverbs to Convey the Correct Meaning

Read the following sentences and observe a mistake in the use of the conjunctive adverbs. Then, answer the questions that follow them.

   a.   Lucia planned on visiting her homeland; *therefore*, she cancelled her trip.

   b.   The college was open; *moreover*, many students were absent because of the snow.

In these sentences, the writer used a conjunctive adverb:

   a.   with the correct meaning.

   b.   with the incorrect meaning.

   c.   instead of a conjunction.

   d.   none of these

Answer [27]

---

[27] If you selected choice <u>b</u>, you are correct

Warning: When you write, be certain to use the conjunctive adverb that states the intended meaning. The following chart specifies the meaning of these words.

Meaning of Conjunctive Adverbs

Review the following chart to clarify the precise meaning of some commonly *misused* conjunctive adverbs.

To provide **additional** information, use:

in addition   moreover   furthermore   additionally   besides

To provide an **unexpected result** or a **contrast**, use:

however   in contrast   nevertheless   conversely   nonetheless

To demonstrate a **result** or **consequence**, use:

therefore   hence   consequently   thus   as a consequence

as a result

Controlled Practice

Connect the following sentences using conjunctive adverbs. If there are three main clauses, be certain to apply the rules just learned so that your compound sentences only contain two main clauses.

e.g.   The doctor explained the dietary restrictions to his patient. The patient ate whatever he wanted anyway.

The doctor explained the dietary restrictions to his patient; however, the patient ate whatever he wanted anyway.

1. The builder ran out of money. He was unable to finish constructing our house.

_____

2. The police claimed the suspect was driving under the influence of alcohol. A blood alcohol test revealed that his blood contained no alcohol.

_____

3. Juan-Carlos failed three exams. He was absent ten times. The professor gave him a failing grade.

4. We were informed that the house had termites. We didn't purchase it.

_____

5. Our professor was absent yesterday. We had class with a substitute instructor.

_____

6. My professor was sick yesterday. Our class was cancelled.

_____

7. The man was driving and talking on a cell phone. He received a ticket.

_____

8. We had twelve inches of snow. The college was closed.

_____

9. We had twelve inches of snow. The college was still open yesterday.

_____

10. The hurricane tore the roof off the house. It flooded our basement.

_____

Error Analysis

Read the following composition and edit it for errors:

- in the connection of main and reduced clauses,
- use of conjunctive adverbs, and
- use of conjunctions and conjunctive adverbs that convey the correct meaning.

When I was in college, I worked part time as a bank teller, therefore I also took a sixteen credits in college. Although this job didn't pay well, I think it was my favorite job because it was fun and convenient.

The bank that I worked at was located only three blocks from my apartment, however I was able to walk to work. I never had to wait for a bus or pay car fare, and the trip to work only took five minutes. In contrast, when I worked at a mall, I had to take a bus. I sometimes waited thirty minutes just for the bus to arrive. Then, if the bus had no room for passengers, I had to wait for the next bus. Additionally, it took me an hour just to get to the mall.

On the other hand, I liked this job because a lot of young people worked at the bank. Moreover, I made lots of new friends. On weekends, after we finished work, we would go out to the movies or have something to eat. Additionally, when I worked at the mall, I didn't make any friends. The people were nice; besides, we had nothing in common. In fact, most of the employees were married adults with families. Therefore, the job at the mall didn't provide any social outlets, but the days seemed endless.

However, the work I did at the bank was interesting, too. We had to interact with the public politely and effectively, even if the customers were not courteous to us. In contrast, we had to be careful not make any mistakes with the money we handled, for we had to "prove up" at the end of the day to verify that we hadn't made any errors. For a college student, these demands seemed overwhelming, and they taught me how to function in the business world.

Clearly, working at the bank assisted me in developing many financial, social and business skills; on the other hand, it also permitted me to enjoy meeting new people.

Practice Writing

Write a composition describing one of the following situations:

- a job you enjoyed, or

- a job you disliked, or

- your idea of a perfect job.

Be certain to connect your main and reduced clauses correctly.

Dependent Adverbial Clauses

In this chapter, you will learn about dependent adverbial clauses and how to connect them to main clauses.

Read the following statements and answer the questions below.

a. If I were twenty-one years old

b. When I lived in my country

c. Before Ella enrolled in college

d. As soon as I finish my homework

Are these statements complete sentences? Yes or No Answer [1]

These four statements are all _____ :

a. dependent adverbial clauses

b. main clauses

c. adjective clauses

d. prepositional phrases

Answer [2]

Dependent adverbial clauses:

a. can stand alone as a sentence in English.

b. are not sentences because they make no sense by themselves.

c. are a highly complex structures that ESL students should avoid using.

d. all of these

Answer [3]

When an adverbial clause stands alone, it is called a:

a. run on sentence

b. fragment

c. comma splice

d. complete sentence

Answer [4]

---

[1] No, these are not sentences. They are fragments.
[2] If you selected choice a, you are correct.
[3] If you selected choice b, you are correct
[4] If you selected choice b, you are correct.

Read each of the following sentences, and label the main clause (MC) and the dependent clause (DC), as in the example.

  DC   MC
a. Before I came to class, I went to the library.

  MC   DC
b. I went to the library, before I came to class.

1. a. My family moved to this country, when I was 17 years old.

    b. When I was 17 years old, my family moved to this country.

2. a. As I was walking in the door, I heard someone scream.

    b. I heard someone scream, as I was walking in the door.

3. a. Maria bought a new car, after she won the lottery.

    b. After Maria won the lottery, she bought a new car.

In these sentence pairs, the adverbial clauses can:

    a. be placed before the main clause.

    b. be placed after the main clause.

    c. stand by itself as a sentence

    d. a and b

Answer [5]

Adverbial clauses are unique from other clauses because:

    a. they can be moved to the beginning or the end of a sentence.

    b they can stand alone and function as a complete sentence.

    c. they must be placed immediately after the noun the clause is modifying.

    d. all of these

Answer [6]

Read the following sentences, and observe what punctuation mark is used to separate the adverbial clause from the main clause.

Until Anoush arrived in Los Angeles, she had never spoken English.

Anoush had never spoken English, until she arrived in New York.

In the sentences listed above, the adverbial clauses are separated from the main clauses with a _____. Answer [7]

Placement and Punctuation of Adverbial Clauses
Adverbial Clauses can be placed at the beginning or the end of a sentence, and are separated from the main clause with a comma.
e.g. I go to work, after my class ends.   After my class ends, I go to work.

---

[5] If you selected choice <u>d</u>, you are correct.
[6] If you selected choice <u>a</u>, you are correct.
[7] comma

Adverbial clauses begin with a special word called a:

a. conjunction

b. subordinating conjunction

c. relative pronoun

d. danger word

e. b and d

Answer [8]

Subordinating conjunctions are also called *danger words* because if they are used incorrectly, you might create a _____ **.** Answer [9]

Can you try to create a list of danger words?

_____ _____ _____ _____

_____ _____ _____ _____

_____ _____ _____ _____

_____ _____ _____ _____

_____ _____ _____ _____

_____ _____ _____ _____

Read the following sentence to determine what has bee done incorrectly.

(incorrect →) Because, Adriana ran a red light, she received a $250 fine.

This sentence is grammatically incorrect, because the writer:

a. placed a comma after a subordinating conjunction (danger word).

b. created a fragment.

c. treated a subordinating conjunction as though it were a conjunction or a conjunctive adverb.

d. a and c

Answer [10]

---

[8] If you selected choice e, you are correct.
[9] fragment

Subordinating Conjunctions

Adverbial clauses begin with subordinating conjunctions, which are also called danger words.

Some commonly used subordinating conjunctions are:

after	although	as	even if
before	even though	so that	provided that
during	because	such that	as long as
when	every time	in order to	since
until	whenever	where as	if
while	inasmuch as	wherever	the first time that
though	once	even when	whether
especially	especially when	as soon as	despite
instead of	especially since	because of	in spite of

Note: never place a comma after a conjunctive adverb.

e.g. (incorrect →) Because**,** Mariska was sad, she was smiling.

(correct →) Because Mariska was sad, she was smiling.

Read the following sentences. Circle *each* adverbial clause and state in the first column the number of adverbial clauses each sentence contains. The first sentence has been done for your.

Number of Adverbial Clauses		
3	1.	When Louisa was a young woman, she worked full time, while she attended college at night because she couldn't afford to be a full time student.
	2.	If Tracey marries Chang, she can't pursue her career, because he doesn't want her to work when they have children.
	3.	Although I agreed to help Jiang write his paper because English is his second language, I didn't give him much guidance, because I was too busy.
	4.	Even though the instructor was absent because he had a death in his family, the students met in order to practice for their final exam since the test was so difficult.
	5.	When Lorena was already a thirty-years-old mother because she still didn't have a driver's license, she took driving lessons every week, unt[il] she finally passed the test because she had to drive her children back and forth to school

In the previous chapter, you learned that one sentence can only contain two main clauses. In contrast, one sentence can contain:

   a. several adverbial clauses, as long as the sentence does not become difficult to understand.
   b. no more than two adverbial clauses.
   c. no adverbial clauses.
   d. none of these.

Answer [11]

Controlled Practice

With a partner, complete each of the following sentences by attaching a main clause to the adverbial clause provided. Be certain to keep the verb tenses consistent. For instance if the adverbial clause is in the past tense, typically the verb in the main clause will use the past tense, too.

e.g.   Even though Jose liked living in Texas, _____.

---

[11] If you selected choice a, you are correct.

Even though Jose liked living in Texas, *he moved to Florida for a better job opportunity.*

1. When we arrived at the airport, _____.

2. _____, as soon as I receive my college degree.

3. Because Wei had a toothache, _____.

4. When Alejandra spilled grape juice on the teacher's desk, _____ _____.

5. _____, if they knew how to drive.

6. Even if the students attend every class, _____.

7. _____, while I was reading a book last night.

8. _____, until you stop creating fragments!

9. _____ because Zlata married Peter.

10. _____, such as pens, pencils, notebooks and paper.

Practice

With a partner, write five sentences that contain one main clause and at least one adverbial clause about your classes, school, job, family or friends. Refer to the list of subordinating conjunctions to create these sentences.

e.g. *When students arrive late for class, our professor gets annoyed because she thinks they will fail, even though some of these students write well.*

1. _____
   _____
   _____

2. _____
   _____
   _____

3. _____
   _____
   _____

4. _____
   _____
   _____

5. _____
   _____
   _____

Error Analysis

Read the following composition carefully and locate any fragments. Then connect these fragments to main clauses. Be certain to connect each adverbial clause to the main clause to which it is logically related.

For years, when dentists have discovered cavities. They have drilled away the rotted enamel, and filled the cavity. In order to prevent additional tooth decay. However, even a small amount of drilling for a tiny cavity can destroy healthy enamel on the tooth. Although, dentists try to limit the damage, even the most skilled dentist is forced to destroy a large amount of the tooth to create a surface big enough for the filling.

However, Japanese researchers believe that they have discovered a new way to treat cavities by painting a special mixture on a tooth. Instead of drilling it. Dr.

Yamagishi said this mixture is composed of fluorine ions, hydroxyapatite (the crystalline material of tooth enamel) and acid that dissolves into a paste. After this paste is applied to a cavity. The material hardens and forms a seamless bond. Moreover, because, the paste contains fluorine. It protects against tooth decay. Even when this mixture is placed on a tooth and viewed with a microscope. No visible gap or space exists between the tooth and this mixture. Moreover, because this paste grows crystals that attach well to a tooth. It becomes a natural part of the tooth. Especially since the white paste blends well with the natural color of the tooth.

Presently this special mixture has only been tested on small cavities. Therefore, before, this paste can be used commercially by dentists. It is necessary to study it further. In order to confirm its safety.

Practice Writing

1. Paragraph Writing

After editing the previous passage about the new paste developed to treat cavities, write a paragraph explaining why you think this new formula will or will not revolutionize the treatment of cavities. In this paragraph, be certain to include several sentences that contain adverbial clauses connected to main clauses. After you write the paragraph, proofread it to verify that there are no fragments.

e.g. *Many people avoid getting their cavities treated because they dread having their teeth drilled. Therefore, ...*

_____

_____

_____

_____

_____

_____

_____

2. Composition Writing

Write a composition about one of the following topics:

- explain why some people fear getting their teeth drilled at the dentist and how this new treatment could eliminate this fear, or

- describe a time you or a friend had a negative experience in a dentist's office.

In this composition, be certain to include several sentences in each paragraph that contain adverbial clauses that are connected to main clauses. After you write the composition, proofread it to verify that there are no fragments.

Adverbial Clauses of Reason and Contrast

Read each of the following sentence pairs and underline the adverbial clause.

1. a. Marcia left work early because she felt sick.

   b. Marcia left work early since she felt sick.

   c. Marcia left work early inasmuch as she felt sick.

2. a. Bing was late for class because he missed his bus.

   b. Bing was late for class since he missed his bus.

   c. Bing was late for class inasmuch as he missed his bus.

Each of these adverbial clauses provides a _____ .

   a. conditional statement

   b. contrast or unexpected result

   c. reason

   d. b and c

Answer [12]

_____

[12] If you selected choice c, you are correct.

An adverbial clause of reason can begin with the following subordinating conjunctions:

    a. and

    b. because

    c. since

    d. inasmuch as

    e. all of these

    f. b, c and d.

Answer [13]

Adverbial Clauses of Reason

An adverbial clause of reason provides an explanation for the information discussed in the main clause. Adverbial clauses of reason use the following subordinating conjunctions.

    because   **since**   **inasmuch as**

e.g. Because he was rich and famous, many women liked him.

      I missed the lecture since I was out of town.

      We can't attend the party, inasmuch as we have other plans.

Controlled Practice

With a partner, combine each of the following sentences so that the main clause that provides a reason becomes an adverbial clause of reason that begins with *because, since, or inasmuch as*.

e.g.   Maurice missed ten classes. He failed the test.

      Because Maurice missed ten classes, he failed the test.

1.   The women had been on strict diets. They were very hungry.

    _____

---

[13] If you selected choice f, you are correct.

2. The burglar entered the house with ease. The window was unlocked.

_____

_____

3. My CD player wouldn't work. The batteries were dead.

_____

_____

4. The driver lost control of his car. He was talking on a cell phone.

_____

_____

5. The elderly woman fainted. Her daughter called an ambulance.

_____

_____

6. The airport was closed for three days. A blizzard had dumped 24 inches of snow on the City.

_____

_____

7. Irina went to the library. She needed a quiet place to study.

_____

_____

8. Marina loves baseball. She bought season tickets for the Yankees.

_____

_____

9. Bill checks his stock portfolio daily. He wants to get rich and retire.

_____

_____

10. That teacher required us to read three novels. She wanted us to improve our reading skills.

_____

_____

Practice Writing

Write three sentences about your class that contain three adverbial clauses of reason using because, since, and inasmuch as.

e.g.   *I took this class because it fit into my schedule.*

1. _____

_____

2. _____

_____

3. _____

_____

Expressing a Contrast in an Adverbial Clause

What is a contrast? A contrast expresses a/an:

 a. expected outcome.

 b. unexpected result.

 c. conditional result.

 d. all of these.

Answer [14]

Therefore, an adverbial clause of contrast expresses an _____ result.

Answer [15]

Read each of the following sentence pairs and underline the adverbial clause of contrast.

1. a. Although Marco usually makes a great meal, his roast beef was dry.

 b. Even though Marco usually makes a great meal, his roast beef was dry.

2. a. Even though it was hot, the old woman was wearing a winter coat.

 b. Although it was hot, the old woman was wearing a winter coal.

---

[14] If you selected choice <u>b</u>, you are correct
[15] unexpected or unanticipated

Each of these adverbial clauses provide a _____.

   a. conditional statement

   b. reason

   c. contrast

   d. b and c

Answer [16]

A contrast can also be expressed with the subordinating conjunction *despite*; however, this danger word is usually followed by a noun, as in the following example.

   Despite Diana's effort, she still didn't understand the math problem.

   Despite Julisa's love for Tomas, she couldn't marry him.

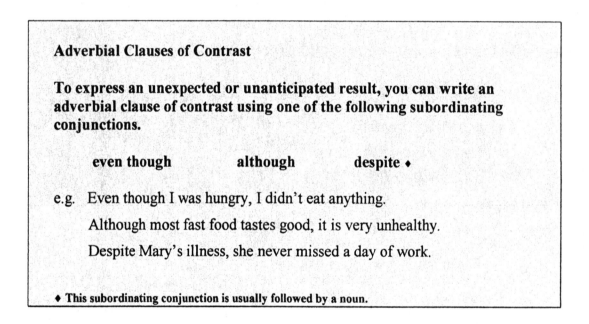

Adverbial Clauses of Contrast

To express an unexpected or unanticipated result, you can write an adverbial clause of contrast using one of the following subordinating conjunctions.

     even though   **although**   **despite** ♦

e.g. Even though I was hungry, I didn't eat anything.

      Although most fast food tastes good, it is very unhealthy.

      Despite Mary's illness, she never missed a day of work.

♦ This subordinating conjunction is usually followed by a noun.

Controlled Practice

With a partner, combine each of the following sentences, and make the sentence that provides the unexpected or unanticipated result an adverbial clause of contrast that begins with *even though, although or despite*.

e.g.   Jean Pierre missed many classes. He still received an A in the course.

       Even though Jean Pierre missed many classes, he still received an A in the course.

---

[16] If you selected choice c, you are correct.

196

1. Larisa wasn't feeling well. She went to church on Sunday.

   _____

   _____

2. No one has ever entered Mrs. Sturgis' house illegally. She never locks her doors.

   _____

   _____

3. My television is brand new. It doesn't work.

   _____

   _____

4. Marisa likes Paolo. She refused to date him.

   _____

   _____

5. Frank had a nice warm coat. He didn't wear it when it snowed.

   _____

   _____

6. The children went ice-skating. The sign at the lake said, "No Ice Skating."

   _____

   _____

7. Clara missed her train yesterday. She arrived at work early.

   _____

   _____

8. Sean is extremely handsome. No one likes him because he is mean.

   _____

   _____

9. Sarita didn't do her job well and was late frequently. She was given a promotion.

   _____

   _____

10. Many students failed the physics test. They studied a lot.

    _____

    _____

Practice Writing

Write three sentences about your best friend, siblings or parents that use adverbial clauses of *contrast* and the subordinating conjunctions *even though, although or despite*.

e.g. *My husband and I went to Florida during the summer even though we don't like the hot humid weather.*

Although my cousin wanted to attend college, she couldn't afford the tuition.

1. _____

_____

2. _____

_____

3. _____

_____

Controlled Contextualized Practice

Read the following passage and select the correct subordinating conjunction of reason or contrast, depending on the meaning expressed in the sentence.

Two graduate economics students, recently discovered that **(since, even though)** Americans use their cell phones more often when they drive their cars, they are not involved in more automobile accidents. They found that **(because of, despite)** the fact that forty percent of Americans use their cell phones while driving, the number of fatal and non-fatal accidents has decreased or remained consistent from 1987 to 2005. These researchers concluded that talking on a cell phone is no more distracting or dangerous than many of the other activities American conduct while driving, **(inasmuch as, although)** these statistics contradict what many people intuitively believe about cell phones and car accidents.

Research from the National Highway Traffic Safety Administration demonstrated that the vast majority of accidents could be prevented if drivers simply paid more attention to the road. Another study conducted by Nationwide Insurance indicated that distracted driving is a national pastime in the United States **(since, even though)** approximately three quarters of those questioned reported that they use a cell phone while driving. In addition, many people stated they eat while driving, while others shave, apply makeup, read, and even paint their toenails in traffic, **(because, although)** teenagers appear to be the most easily sidetracked behind the wheel. More than half of the teens polled said they saw other teens driving while text messaging or using handheld games. These young drivers are a major concern **(since, even though)** they are the least experienced drivers and are more likely to be involved serious accidents.

Many drivers don't view these distractions as a risk, **(inasmuch as, although)** their activities don't always result in accidents, but accidents occur when the situation behind the wheel of a car changes rapidly. When a driver is distracted, he/she misses warning signals, **(because, although)** unfocused drivers don't detect visual cues **(since, even though)** they don't see the situation developing. For example, if a driver is attentive, it's easy to see a ball roll into the street and to predict a child may be running behind it; however, if the driver is dialing a phone or glancing down to pick up a cup of hot coffee, the driver might hit the child **(because, although)** he/she has missed an important warning signal.

(Since, although) many people also equate talking on a cell phone with chatting with other people in the car, passengers in the car are aware of what is transpiring on the road and modify their conversation accordingly. In contrast, **(because, even though)** the party on the other end of the cell phone can't see the traffic, it is unlikely that he/she will pause when an alarming situation develops.

In recent years, over fifty countries have adopted laws banning the use of hand-held phones while driving, **(because, despite the fact)** cell phone conversations may only be one of the many diversions behind the wheel of a car. If this is true, many of these laws may be ineffective **(inasmuch as, although)** these regulations don't eliminate all the disruptions drivers participate.

Practice Writing
Select one of the following topics to write a composition.

1. Write a composition explaining why you think drivers should or should not be permitted to talk on cell phones or send text messages while they are driving.

2. Write a composition describing a time you witnessed or heard about an accident that resulted when a driver was talking or texting on a cell phone or performing some other distracting activity while driving.

Conditional Clauses

In the previous chapter, you learned to create dependent adverbial clauses. In this chapter, you will learn how to create conditional adverbial clauses, which are formed by following some unusual, but simple rules.

Read each of the following sentences, and answer the questions that follow.

1. a. If Alla <u>works</u> on Friday, she <u>will bring</u> the donuts and coffee.

    b. If Alla <u>worked</u> on Friday, she <u>would bring</u> the donuts and coffee.

2. a. If we <u>go</u> to the museum, you <u>can join</u> us.

    b. If we <u>went</u> to the museum, you <u>could join</u> us.

3. a. If Lydia <u>marries</u> Arthur, she <u>will be</u> very happy.

    b. If Lydia <u>married</u> Arthur, she <u>would be</u> very happy.

A conditional adverbial clause can begin with the subordinating conjunction ____.

Answer [1]

In the above sentences pairs:

a. letter <u>a</u> express a present tense situation, and letter <u>b</u> describes a past situation.

b. letter <u>a</u> describes a possible or true situation, but letter <u>b</u> expresses a present situation that is not likely to occur or is unrealistic or untrue.

c. letter <u>a</u> contains a fragment that must be connected to a main clause.

d. a and c

Answer [2]

Understanding the Meaning of Conditional Clauses

Read the following sentences, and answer the true/false questions that follow.

a. If Yelena <u>studies</u> harder, she <u>will pass</u> her psychology course.

b. If Yelena <u>studied</u> harder, she <u>would pass</u> her psychology course.

---

[1] if
[2] If you selected choice <u>b</u>, you are correct.

True False	1.	In letter <u>a</u>, it is possible that Yelena will study harder, and pass the class.
True False	2.	Letter <u>b</u> suggests that Yelena will pass the course.
True False	3.	Letter <u>b</u> implies that it is highly unlikely that Yelena is going to study harder. Therefore, it is doubtful she will pass the class.

Answers [3]

Forming Conditional Sentences

Can you state the rule for writing *true* conditional and result clauses?

Conditional *IF* Clause   ***Result* Clause**

If + subject + _____,   **_____ + will or can + _____**

Answer [4]

Can you write a sentence, using this rule?

_____

Can you state the rule for writing *untrue* conditional and result clauses?

Conditional *IF* Clause   ***Result* Clause**

If + subject + _____,   **subject + _____ + simple form of the verb**

Answer [5]

Can you write a sentence, using this rule?

_____

---

[3] Number 1 is true. Number 2 is false. Number 3 is true.
[4] If + subject + present tense of verb, subject + will or can + simple form of the verb
[5] If + subject + past tense of verb, subject + would or could + simple form of the verb

Untrue Conditional Clauses and the Verb *To Be*

Each of the following statements is grammatically correct, but something unusual occurs. Read the following sentences, and observe the form of the verb *to be* in an untrue conditional if statement.

If **I** *were* a nurse, I would take care of my aunt.

If **you** *were* hungry, you would eat dinner.

If **she** *were* sociable, she would have more friends.

If **he** *were* at the football game, he would have fun.

If **it** *were* cold today, I would wear a coat, hat and gloves.

If **we** *were* in class, we would know that answer.

If **they** *were* in love, they would get married.

When you use the verb *to be* in an untrue present conditional clause, the verb:

   a.   strictly follows the rules of present tense subject-verb agreement.

   b.   breaks the rules of subject verb agreement and always uses *were*, when the subject is *I, he, she* or *it*.

   c.   uses *was* when the subject is *I, he, she* or *it*.

   d.   a and c

Answer [6]

In contrast, read the following true conditional sentences that use the verb *to be*.

   If I am late, I will get in trouble.

   If she is hungry, she can eat a piece of fruit.

   If it rains, the picnic will be postponed.

When you use the verb *to be* in a true conditional sentence, the verb:

   a.   strictly follows the rules of present tense subject verb agreement.

   b.   breaks the rules of present tense subject verb agreement when the subject is *I, he, she* or *it*.

   c.   uses *was* when the subject is *I, he, she* or *it*.

   d.   a and c

Answer [7]

---

[6] If you selected choice <u>b</u>, you are correct.

[7] If you selected choice <u>a</u>, you are correct.

Present Conditional Clauses

Present conditional clauses express whether an event might possibly occur. This distinction is made by changing the tenses. In *present true* conditional sentences, use the following form.

If Clause	**Result Clause**
If + subject + present, tense	subject + will or + simple form can of the verb

e.g. If Ignazia pays her mortgage on time, she will keep her house.

If the situation is *untrue* or unlikely to occur, use the following form.

If Clause	**Result Clause**
If + subject + past, tense	subject + would or + simple form could of the verb

e.g. If Ignazia paid her mortgage on time, she could keep her house.

However, if the verb *to be* is used in an untrue conditional statement, the rule for subject verb agreement is broken, so that you must use *were*, when the subject is *I, he, she* or *it*.

e.g.   If I *were* satisfied, I would not complain.
          If he *were* wise, he would call her tonight.
          If she *were* happy, she wouldn't cry.
          If it *were* a nice day, we would go to the baseball game.

Controlled Practice

With a partner, read each of the following statements and complete the sentences with the correct conditional form, depending on whether the situation is possible and true, or unlikely and untrue.

1. I am thinking about purchasing a new computer.

    If I (purchase) _____ a new computer, I (buy) _____ a laptop.

2. I don't need a new computer because I just bought one.

    If I (purchase) _____ a new computer, I (buy) _____ a printer, too.

3. Ludmila doesn't plan to go to Israel this year.

If Ludmila (travel) _____ to Israel this summer, she (visit) _____ Jerusalem.

4. I am 42 years old.

   If I (be) _____ 65 years old, I (retire) _____.

5. Lisa and Sara are about to turn 18 years old.

   If Lisa and Sara (be) _____ 18 years old, they (drive) _____ a car without an adult present.

6. Franco doesn't have an extra ticket to the opera.

   If Franco (have) _____ an extra ticket to the opera, he (give) _____ it to Patrizio.

7. You don't play the piano well.

   If you (play) _____ well, everyone (enjoy) _____ listening the music.

8. We sing well.

   If we (sing) _____ well, we (try) _____ out for the talent show.

9. You won't go to the movies tonight.

   If you (go) _____ to the movies, you (invite) _____ a friend.

10. Tina dances very well.

    If Tina (dance) _____ in the contest, she (win) _____ first prize.

Practice Writing

Complete each of the following statements using the correct conditional form. Be certain to examine the verb first to determine whether the situation is true or untrue so that you use the correct conditional form.

e.g.   If I get home early, I _____. (←present true conditional)
        If I get home early, *I will take a nap.*

        I would buy a new car, if _____.(←present untrue conditional)
        I would buy a new car, if *I had enough money.*

1. If Jose and I win the new car, _____.

2. If Anibol won the lottery, _____.

3. I can buy a new coat next year if _____.

4. If my parents travel to Spain, _____.

5. My parents would be angry if _____.

6. The doctors could help him if _____.

7. If Louisa married Paul, _____.

8. _____ if the instructor answers my questions.

9. If _____, you can arrive at work early.

10. You could lose weight if _____.

11. My husband/wife would kill me if _____.

12. _____, if a student never attends class.

13. If they got engaged, _____.

14. If Elsa and Matteo have disagreement about money, _____.

15. If _____, the teacher will miss our class.

16. If a student copies a paper off the Internet and the teacher finds out, _____
_____

17. If a medical school student cheated on his/her exams, _____.

18. Her parents would believe her if _____.

19. If _____, I could buy a house for my family.

20. If Monica doesn't buy the gift, _____.

Practice Writing

1. Congratulations! You just found out that you and your spouse are having a baby boy. Write a conditional clause explaining what you will name the baby if you have a boy.

   If _____, _____.

2. You are only earning $15,000 a year. Write a conditional clause explaining what you would do if you earned $500,000 a year.

   If _____, _____.

Practice in Context

Read the following health information. Next, after each recommendation, write two conditional if statements: one to describe what a person can do to prevent a heart attack (present true conditional) and one to describe what could occur if this person doesn't follow this recommendation (present untrue conditional). The first is done for you.

1. Walking for thirty minutes each day reduces the risk of having a heart attack by about thirty percent. Moreover, research shows that if people succeed at walking every day, they can also find other ways to improve their health. However, when they stop walking, they compromise their health.

   true   *If I walk with my husband for 30 minutes every day, I can reduce my risk of having a heart attack.*

   untrue *If I refused to exercise daily, I would increase my chances of having a heart attack.*

2. A normal blood pressure level is approximately 115/75. Some doctors believe blood pressure is more important than cholesterol levels. People can lower their blood pressure by getting a little exercise and losing some weight, especially around the stomach area because the fat that hangs over the stomach nourishes the kidney, liver and other vital organs. Therefore, when you lose just a few pounds, your blood pressure decreases quickly. Reducing salt intake can also reduce blood pressure.

   true   _____

   _____

   untrue _____

   _____

3. Consuming one ounce of nuts each day can raise HDL, which is known as good cholesterol. But nuts also benefit the heart, although it is not known why. Nuts contain healthy omega-three fatty acids, healthy protein and some fiber. But, it is important to eat nuts that are raw, fresh and unsalted because they offer the most benefits. When you want to eat roasted nuts, cook them in the oven at 350 degrees for about ten minutes because this cooking method does not cause the development of bad fats or dangerous chemicals to form.

true _____

_____

untrue _____

_____

4. It is important to know your HDL number and to raise it to fifty. Some research suggests that in women a high HDL is more important than a lower LDL, the bad cholesterol. Once again, the reason for this effect is unknown, but study after study shows that the higher the HDL, the better. You can increase your HDL by exercising, having one drink a day, and eating healthy fats such as olive oil and nuts.

true _____

_____

untrue _____

_____

5. Tomato sauce also lowers blood pressure. It is suggested adults eat ten tablespoons of tomato sauce a week because it is rich with blood-pressure-slashing potassium. However, avoid salty or fatty sauces, or a huge portion of pasta because these will raise your blood pressure and your LDL.

true _____

_____

untrue _____

_____

6. Read labels and do not consume foods that specify sugar as one of the first five ingredients. Some foods are low in fat but high in sugar, so that they should be avoided because sugar causes inflammations and gets morphed into the dangerous fat around the belly. Some low fat salad dressings are filled with calories and sugar so they should also be avoided.

true _____

_____

untrue _____

_____

Past Conditional Situations

You just learned how to express present conditional true and untrue statements. Now you will learn to create **Past Untrue Conditional Statements**.

Read the following sentences, and observe the meaning and the form of the past conditional untrue sentences.

1. If Oksana <u>had attended</u> her classes, she <u>could have received</u> a good grade.

2. If we <u>had understood</u> the math problem, we <u>would have solved</u> it.

3. If he <u>had heard</u> the weather report, he <u>would have stayed</u> home.

In these sentences, the writer is expressing:

    a. what he/she would have done at a time in the past.

    b. what he/she might do in the present time.

    c. how a present situation could be modified.

    d. all of these

Answer [8]

In a past untrue situation, the _____ tense is used in the conditional *if* clause. Answer [9]

Select the rule used to form the result clause in a conditional past untrue sentence.

    a. subject + past tense of the verb.

    b. subject + would or could + simple form of the verb

    c. subject + would or could + have + past participle of the verb

    d. none of these

Answer [10]

---

[8] If you selected choice <u>a</u>, you are correct.
[9] past perfect
[10] If you selected choice <u>c</u>, you are correct.

Past Untrue Conditional Clauses

Past untrue conditional statements are created by using the following form.

	If Clause		Result Clause		
If + subject +	past perfect, tense	subject +	would or could	+ have +	past participle to be (been)

e.g. If Lucia had married Carlos, she would have been rich.
If we had been older, we could have purchased the car.

Controlled Practice

With a partner, read each of the following statements, and then complete it with the correct form of the past untrue conditional.

1. I wanted to buy a new television last week.

   If I (purchase) _____ a new flat screen television last week, I (save) _____ a lot of money because it was on sale.

2. Karina didn't answer the text message because her phone was turned off.

   Karina (respond) _____ to the text message, if she (turn) _____ on her cell phone.

3. We didn't know your grandmother had heart surgery.

   If we (know) _____ about your grandmother's surgery, we (visit) _____ her in the hospital

4. Yvette and Tomas always consumed a lot of fried food and sweets.

   If Yvette and Tomas (maintain) _____ a more healthy diet, their blood pressure (be) _____ lower.

5. Because the students didn't know their instructor was sick, they arrived for their class early in the morning.

   If the students (know) _____ about their teacher's illness, they (not, come) _____ so early.

Practice Writing

Complete each of the following statements using the correct conditional form, but be certain to examine the verb to determine whether the situation is present true, present untrue or past untrue.

e.g.   If I had done my research paper well, I _____.(←past untrue)
    If I had done my research paper well, I *could have received an A in that class.*

    I would study harder, if _____. (←present untrue)
    I would study harder, if *I had the time.*

1. If I were afraid to be alone in the house, _____.

2. If I am afraid to be alone in the house, _____

3. If I had been afraid to be alone in the house, _____.

4. If Svetlana knows what Paolo is like, _____.

5. She wouldn't have trusted him if_____.

6. Those girls would enjoy being with Ariela if _____

    _____.

7. If Alfredo discussed the problem with me, _____

8. _____, if my husband had earned

    more money at that time.

9. If _____, Lucia could have attended a

    private university.

10. Antonio would understand his errors better, if _____

    _____.

11. We will end the class early today, if _____.

12. _____, if a person donates one million

    dollars to the college.

13. If Juanita had lied to Ricardo, _____

    _____.

14. If that teacher had understood teenagers, _____.

15. If _____, we will feed you dinner.

16. If Maria and Jean had taken that plane, _____

_____.

17. If I hadn't warned you about him, _____.

18. My wife/husband would have listened to me, if _____

_____.

19. If my parents had saved enough money, _____.

20. If Maria had a job, _____.

Error Analysis

With a partner, read each of the following paragraphs, which specify present true, present untrue, and past untrue situations. After determining if the situation is present true, present untrue, or past untrue, edit the underlined verbs so that they use the correct conditional form. For instance, if a situation is untrue, use the untrue conditional format.

1. **Situation**: Pedro is a thirty-five year old man who dropped out of college to get married ten years ago. He now regrets leaving college.

   If Pedro knew how much more money he would have earned with a college diploma,

   he would wait until he finished college to get married. If he stayed in college, he

   would have had a nice job as an accountant. He can work in a nice clean office, and

   would have earned a lot more money. His life would have been much easier.

2. **Situation**: Lara is about to graduate from high school, and she wants to take a vacation, get a job and go to college after her graduation

   If Lara graduates from high school in June, she could take a vacation with some of

   her friends. She wants to visit California for a few weeks. However, if she took a

   vacation, she will not be home for about a month so that she couldn't set up job

   interviews. Moreover, if she goes on a trip, she can't enroll in summer school courses at the local community college. On the other hand, if she <u>started</u> to search for a job as soon as she finishes high school, she <u>will be</u> available for summer school and job interviews.

3. **<u>Situation</u>**: In Mavish's culture, the parents arrange marriages for their children. Therefore, she doesn't participate in traditional American dating practices.

If Mavish <u>was</u> American, she <u>could meet</u> young men on her own, and go on dates with them. This <u>will mean</u> that she <u>can decide</u> independently, if she <u>likes</u> a guy or not. Moreover, her parents <u>would not supervise</u> her dates so that Mavish and her boyfriend <u>can go</u> out to dinner or to the movies by themselves. If she <u>fell</u> in love with a nice person, her parents <u>would approve</u> of a love marriage, too.

Practice Writing

1. Try to recall a time when you or a friend made a mistake or had automobile accident or received a traffic ticket. Write a paragraph describing the mistake that was made and the consequences that resulted. Then explain what you would do now, if you could go back in time. (Hint this writing activity requires the use of past untrue conditional statement. e.g. If I hadn't made an illegal right turn, I would not have received a $250 ticket.)

2. Write a paragraph describing an activity you would engage in if you were a very Americanized person. (Hint this requires the use of the present untrue. e.g. If I were an Americanized student, I would question the teacher's authority.)

3. Write paragraph describing what you will do if a certain event occurs such as passing this course, receiving a good job offer, getting engaged, buying a house, etc. (Hint this requires a present true situation. e.g. If Leopold asks Lydia to marry him, he will buy her an engagement ring.)

Adjective Clauses

In the previous chapters, you learned to form and use adverbial clauses. In this chapter, you will learn to create dependent adjective clauses, which are used to modify or describe a noun.

Read each question that follows.

What is an adjective? An adjective:

a. is the name of a person, place or thing.

b. describes or modifies a noun.

c. modifies an verb

d. is a word that describes the action in a sentence.

Answer [1]

Read the first version of this story and circle the adjectives.

I am a single, thirty-two year old woman. I am also an educated professional. I own a condominium. So, what is my problem? I can't seem to meet a man. In fact most men are divorced. When I go out on dates, these men expect me to pay for every outing. Worse yet, several of these gentlemen have asked to move in with me. I can't understand why I'm unable to meet a decent eligible man. What is wrong with me?

Answer [2]

---

[1] If you selected choice <u>b</u>, you are correct.

[2] I am a single, thirty-two year old woman. I am also an educated professional. I own a condominium. So, what is my problem? I can't seem to meet a man. In fact most men are divorced. When I go out on dates, these men expect me to pay for every outing. Worse yet, several of these gentlemen have asked to move in with me. I can't understand why I'm unable to meet a decent eligible man. What is wrong with me?

Read the revised version of this story, and answer the questions that follow.

I am a single, thirty-two year old woman who is attractive and fun loving. I am also an educated professional who holds down a prestigious job that provides me a generous income. I own a condominium, which is located in an upscale urban area. So, what is my problem? I can't seem to meet a man who is on my level and wants to make a fair commitment to me. In fact most men I meet are divorced and in search of a woman who can support them. When I go out on dates, these men who typically cry poverty expect me to pay for every outing. Worse yet, several of these gentlemen who have no plans of making a commitment have asked to move in with me. I can't understand why I'm unable to meet a decent eligible man who is willing to offer me as much as I can offer in a relationship. What is wrong with me?

Which version of this letter is more interesting and descriptive? _____ Answer [3]

The second letter is more enjoyable because it:

   a. is longer and it is always better to write more, even if it is boring.
   b. includes a lot of adverbial clauses.
   c. contains adjective clauses that provide clearer descriptions of the nouns.
   d. all of the above.

Answer [4]

Adjective clauses must be located:
   a. at the beginning of each sentence.
   b. immediately after the noun they modify.
   c. in the end of the sentence.
   d. anywhere the writer desires.

Answer [5]

---

[3] the second version
[4] If you selected choice c, you are correct.
[5] If you selected choice b, you are correct.

Can you circle the adjective clauses in the second letter? Answer [6]

Read the following statements to determine why they are fragments.

The students that passed the exam. (←fragment not a sentence)

The child who was crying. (←fragment not a sentence)

The adults whom I was speaking to. (←fragment, not a sentence)

These sentences are fragments because they:

a. only contain a subject and an adjective clause.

b. are adverbial clauses

c. don't contain a subject.

d. all of these

Answer [7]

Read the following statements. Determine what is done *incorrectly* and answer the question below them.

The women went to the beach who were on vacation. (←incorrect)

The patients were waiting to see a doctor who were very sick. (←incorrect)

The lifeguard ran into the violent ocean waves who saved the children. (←incorrect)

In these sentences, the writer:

a. inserted the verb in the wrong location.

b. did not place the adjective clauses after the nouns that they modified.

c. created perfect, error-free sentences.

d. created fragments.

Answer [8]

---

[6] I am a single, thirty-two year old woman who is attractive and fun loving. I am also an educated professional who holds down a prestigious job that provides me a generous income. I own a condominium, which is located in an upscale urban area. So, what is my problem? I can't seem to meet a man who is on my level and wants to make a fair commitment to me. In fact most men I meet are divorced and in search of a woman who can support them. When I go out on dates, these men who typically cry poverty expect me to pay for every outing. Worse yet, several of these gentlemen who have no plans of making a commitment have asked to move in with me. I can't understand why I'm unable to meet a decent eligible man who is willing to offer me as much as I can offer in a relationship. What is wrong with me?

[7] If you selected choice a, you are correct.

[8] If you selected choice b, you are correct.

216

Can you re-write these three sentences so that the adjective clause are immediately after the noun it is modifying?

1. _____

2. _____

3. _____

Answer [9]

Dependent Adjective Clauses

An adjective clause modifies or describes a noun and must be placed immediately after the noun it modifies. It cannot be moved around.

       ↓ subject ↓ adjective clause   ↓verb ↓adjective
e.g. The shoppers *who waited on line* for an hour were annoyed.

An adjective clause is a dependent clause and cannot stand alone as a sentence. Sometimes new writers create fragments by providing a subject and an adjective clause without a main clause.

e.g.   ↓ subject   ↓ adjective clause
    (fragment→) The teacher *who taught us chemistry*

    (complete   ↓ subject   ↓ adjective clause   ↓verb   ↓ adjective
    sentence →) The teacher *who taught us* chemistry was very helpful.

Read the following sentences. Underline the adjective clauses, and answer the questions that follow.

    a. The child that ran into the street was unsupervised.

    b. The child who ~~she~~ ran into the street was unsupervised.

    c. The book that I was reading belonged to the professor.

    d. The book which I was reading ~~it~~ belonged to the professor.

Answer [10]

---

[9] a. The women <u>who were on vacation</u> went to the beach.
   b. The patients <u>who were very sick</u> were waiting to see a doctor.
   c. The lifeguard <u>who saved the children</u> ran into the violent ocean waves.
[10] a.   The child <u>that ran into the street</u> was unsupervised.
   b.   The child <u>who ~~she~~ ran into the street</u> was unsupervised.
   c.   The book <u>that I was reading</u> belonged to the professor.
   d.   The book <u>which I was reading ~~it~~</u> belonged to the professor.

The special words used to begin an adjective clause are called:

    a. subjects

    b. indefinite pronouns

    c. relative pronouns

    d. demonstrative adjectives

Answer [11]

When writing an adjective clause, you must omit the word:

    a. that refers to the noun being modified. (The girl who ~~she~~ cried was hysterical.)

    b. that demonstrates the action. (The girl who she ~~cried~~ was hysterical.)

    c. that is an adjective (The girl who cried was ~~hysterical~~.)

    d. none of these

Answer [12]

The relative pronouns _____ and _____ can be used when the noun being modified is a person. Answer [13]

The relative pronouns _that_ and _which_ can be used, when the noun being modified is a_____. Answer [14]

Subject Verb Agreement in Adjective Clauses

Read the following sentences. Circle the subject of the sentence, and underline the adjective clause.

    a. Alicia and Pietro who ~~they~~ _are_ my neighbors work at a bank.

    b. Alicia who ~~she~~ _is_ my neighbor works at a bank.

    c. The cat that ~~it~~ _was_ lost belongs to me.

    d. The cats that ~~they~~ _were_ lost belong to me.

Answer [15]

---

[11] If you selected choice c, you are correct.
[12] If you selected choice a, you are correct.
[13] who or that
[14] an object or a thing
[15]   a. Alicia and Pietro who ~~they~~ _are_ my neighbors work at a bank.
       b. Alicia who ~~she~~ _is_ my neighbor works at a bank.
       c. The cat that ~~it~~ _was_ lost belongs to me.
       d. The cats that ~~they~~ _were_ lost belong to me.

In these sentences, when the word omitted from the adjective clause is the subject, the verb in the adjective clause must:

   a. be in the simple form. (The woman who ~~she~~ complain a lot is my aunt.)

   b. use the past participle. (The woman who ~~she~~ complained a lot is my aunt.)

   c. agree with the noun it is modifying. (The woman who ~~she~~ complains a lot is my aunt.)

Answer [16]

Read the following sentences, and answer the questions that follow them.

   a. My neighbors *whom* I will miss ~~them~~ are moving next week.

   b. None of the employees *whom* I know ~~them~~ would lie.

   c. The students *whom* I teach ~~them~~ usually speak several languages.

In these sentences, the relative pronoun *whom* is used:

   a. when the word omitted from the adjective clause is the subject.

   b. when the word omitted from the adjective clause is the object.

   c. the writer wants to sound very formal.

   d. a and b

Answer [17]

Read these sentences and answer the questions that follow them.

   a. My neighbors *who* ~~they~~ are from China speak three languages.

   b. The employee *who* ~~he~~ always criticizes Maria is jealous of her.

   c. The singers *who* ~~they~~ are performing that opera are from our college.

In these sentences, the relative pronoun *who* is used:

   a. when the word omitted from the adjective clause is the subject.

   b. when the word omitted from the adjective clause is the object.

   c. the writer wants to be casual

   d. a and b

Answer [18]

---

[16] If you selected choice <u>c</u>, you are correct

[17] If you selected choice <u>b</u>, you are correct.

[18] If you selected choice <u>a</u>, you are correct.

More on Adjective Clauses

An adjective clause usually begins with a *relative pronoun* that is placed immediately after the noun it is modifying.

        ↓ subject   ↓ relative pronoun who

e.g.   The students *who failed the exam* were very upset.

        ↓ subject   ↓ relative pronoun that

e.g.   The animals *that were in the zoo* lived in cages.

When using an adjective clause in a sentence, omit the word being modified.

e.g.   ↓ subject   ↓ omit word that refers to women

     The women *who* ~~they~~ *taught us to swim* were lifeguards.

       ↓ subject   ↓ omit the word that refers to cats

     The cats *that* ~~they~~ *roam around our block* fight with the dogs.

The relative pronoun *whom* is used when the omitted word is the object of the adjective clause.

          ↓ relative pronoun   ↓object

e.g.   The customers *whom* I have serviced ~~them~~ are satisfied.

The relative pronoun *who* is used when the omitted word is the subject of the adjective clause.

          relative
        pronoun↓ ↓ subject

e.g.   The customers *who* ~~they~~ are dissatisfied usually complain..

If the omitted noun in the adjective clause is the subject, the verb in the adjective clause must agree with the noun it is modifying.

e.g.   ↓ subject   ↓ the verb agrees with the noun *men*

     The men *who* ~~they~~ *drive* to work must pay to park their cars.

       ↓ subject   ↓ the verb agrees with the noun *man*

     The man *who* ~~they~~ *drives* to work must pay to park his car.

Controlled Practice

With a partner, merge each of the following sentences so that the second sentence becomes an adjective clause within the first sentence. Be certain to use the correct relative pronoun and to omit the word that refers to the noun being modified.

e.g.   Ann met Sven for lunch. Ann works at the college.

Ann _who works at the college_ met Sven for lunch.

1. Carlo is Lorena's boyfriend. Carlo is my neighbor.

   _____

2. I asked Louisa to watch the children. The children were playing in the pool.

   _____

3. I asked Louisa to watch the children. I have known Louisa for many years.

   _____

4. Syed left his office early. He works for a computer company.

   _____

5. That old house is for sale. I love that house.

   _____

6. The snow covered the city. The snow was 23 inches deep.

   _____

7. Those children are in the park. The children are playing basketball.

   _____

8. The teenagers saw the thief. The teenagers were frightened.

   _____

9. The pedestrians yelled at the man. The man was driving recklessly.

   _____

10. The shop sells newspapers and candy. The shop is on the corner.

Controlled Practice

With a partner, add an adjective clause after each underlined noun.

e.g.   My <u>sister</u> works at an engineering <u>firm</u>.

My sister *who is an architect* works at an engineering firm *which is located in Florida.*

1. This <u>course</u> requires students to write many <u>compositions</u>.

2. New <u>immigrants</u> must get accustomed to a new culture and <u>language</u>.

3. The use of steroids among <u>athletes</u> is a major <u>problem</u>.

4. The <u>president</u> can veto a new <u>law</u>.

5. The <u>college</u> provides <u>classes</u> on weekends.

Error Analysis

Read each of the following paragraphs and correct any errors in the use of adjective clauses.

1. I had a friend who she was twenty-five years old, but she never had a date because she was chubby and dressed poorly. All the men which she wanted to date avoided her because of her appearance. Finally one of her friends who she is very attractive encouraged her to lose some weight and helped her purchase some clothing that were

more flattering. Now my friend who are nice-looking gets asked out on dates, and she feels a lot better about herself.

2. My friend Pierina who is pretty, but men are rarely interested in her because she intimidates guys who she meet. Pierina doesn't realize that her behavior scares off many men which is very aggressive. Instead, she believes that men really like a strong, powerful woman who control them. So, I guess she will continue to boss around the men she meet and they will continue to avoid her.

3. My brother has never had a girlfriend who is a really nice looking guy. He is a physician in a hospital that is located in San Diego. Because he wanted to meet a woman who she would be compatible with him, he enrolled in an on-line dating service. He was required to pay a fee of $300 and to complete a survey that contained 350 questions that they were very personal. After his application which he had already paid for was processed, the on-line dating service rejected him and refused to return his money. Now my brother is hiring a lawyer who will try to get his money back.

Adjective Clauses as the Object of the Preposition

In English, when you write a prepositional phrase, you usually place a noun or a pronoun after the preposition as in the following example.

↓ preposition ↓ preposition
↓ a noun ↓ pronoun
Marina works <u>in a factory</u> <u>with them.</u>

However, sometimes a preposition is followed by an adjective clause. In such cases, the adjective clause is *the object of the preposition* as in the following examples.

1. a. My neighbors <u>with whom I am friends</u> shoveled my snow.

b My neighbors <u>whom I am friends with</u> shoveled my snow

2. a. The child <u>to whom I spoke</u> is my niece.

    b. The child <u>whom I spoke to</u> is my niece.

3. a. The people <u>at whom he was staring</u> were very loud and rude.

    b. The people <u>whom he was staring at</u> were very loud and rude.

Is there any difference in meaning between letters <u>a</u> and <u>b</u> in these pairs of sentences? _____ Answer [19]

The relative pronoun *whom* is used because:

  a. after a preposition, an object relative pronoun (*whom*) is required.

  b. *who* is the subject relative pronoun and can't follow a preposition.

  c. it sounds better.

  d. a and b

Answer [20]

The only difference between letters <u>a</u> and <u>b</u> is that:

  a. the preposition is positioned at the beginning of the adjective clause in letter <u>a</u>

  b. the preposition is positioned at the end of the adjective clause in letter <u>b</u>

  c. the sentences use two different verb tenses

  d. a and b

Answer [21]

Does it make a difference if the preposition is placed before or after the adjective clause? _____ Answer [22]

---

[19] No
[20] If you selected choice <u>d</u>, you are correct.
[21] If you selected choice <u>d</u>, you are correct.
[22] No

224

What is done incorrectly in the following sentences?

The students with whom we were studying with were in my German class. (←incorrect)

The teenagers at whom they were looking at are my cousins. (←incorrect)

When an adjective clauses is the object of the preposition, it is necessary to:

a.　state the preposition one time.

b.　make the subject and verb agree.

c.　use the relative pronoun *who* instead of whom.

d.　a and c

Answer [23]

What is wrong with the following adjective clause?

The customers who I was talking to want to purchase the chair.

The tourists who I discussed the problem with were unhappy.

This adjective clause:

a.　uses an object relative pronoun when it should use the subject relative pronoun.

b.　uses a subject relative pronoun even though the adjective clause is the object of the preposition to.

c.　includes a preposition even though it should not.

d.　all of these.

Answer [24]

---

[23] If you selected choice a, you are correct.
[24] If you selected choice b, you are correct.

> **Adjective Clauses as the Object of the Preposition**
>
> **An adjective clause can be the object of a preposition.**
>
>
>
> adjective clause as   main
> ↓ subject   object of the preposition   ↓verb
>
>
> e.g.   The shoppers *with whom I was talking* were complaining about the long line.
>
> **When the adjective clause is the object of the preposition, the preposition can be located before or after the adjective clause. However, only state the preposition *once*.**
>
> e.g. The hospital workers ***with** whom I spoke* were demanding more money.
>   The hospital workers *whom I spoke **with*** were demanding more money.
>
> **When the adjective clause is the object of the preposition, and the noun being modified is a person, use the object relative pronoun *whom*.**
>
> e.g.   (incorrect→)   The woman ~~who~~ I waved at is my mother.
>   (correct→)   The woman whom I waved at is my mother.

Read the following sentences and answer the questions that follow.

1. a.   The police officer <u>to whom I spoke</u> is my brother.

    b.   The police officer <u>whom I spoke to</u> is my brother.

    c.   The police officer <u>I spoke to</u> is my brother.

In letter <u>c</u>, the relative pronoun *whom* was omitted because:

    a.   the adjective clause is the object of the preposition and the preposition is placed at the end of the adjective clause.

    b.   the preposition is placed in the front of the adjective clause.

    c.   the writer wanted to write a very short sentence.

    d.   a and c

Answer [25]

---

[25] If you selected choice <u>a</u>, you are correct.

Read the following sentences and answer the question that follows.

a. The house <u>which I bought ~~it~~</u> is new.

b. The house <u>that I bought ~~it~~</u> is new.

c. The house <u>I bought ~~it~~</u> is new.

The relative pronoun can be omitted in letter <u>c</u> because:

a. the adjective clause is the object of the preposition.

b. the word omitted in the adjective clause (it) is the subject of the adjective clause.

c. the word omitted in the adjective clause (it) is the object of the adjective clause.

d. none of these

Answer [26]

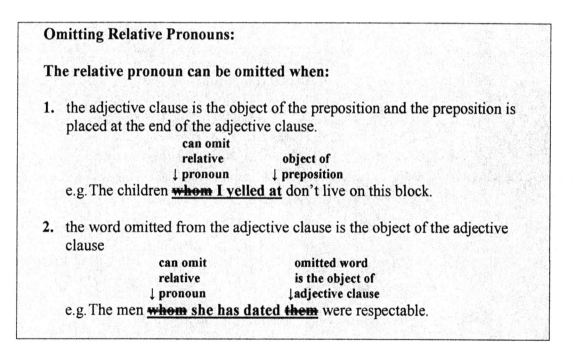

Omitting Relative Pronouns:

The relative pronoun can be omitted when:

1. the adjective clause is the object of the preposition and the preposition is placed at the end of the adjective clause.

        can omit
        relative   object of
        ↓ pronoun   ↓ preposition

   e.g. The children ~~whom~~ **I yelled at** don't live on this block.

2. the word omitted from the adjective clause is the object of the adjective clause

        can omit   omitted word
        relative   is the object of
        ↓ pronoun   ↓adjective clause

   e.g. The men ~~whom~~ **she has dated** ~~them~~ were respectable.

Controlled Practice

With a partner, merge each of the following sentences so that the second sentence becomes an adjective clause that is the object of the preposition in the first sentence. Be certain to use the correct relative pronoun and to omit the word that refers to the noun being modified.

---

[26] If you selected choice <u>c</u>, you are correct.

e.g.　The children were from another country. They were playing with each other.

　　　The children *with whom they were playing* were from another country.
　　　The children *they were playing with* were from another country.
　　　The children *whom they were playing with* were from another country.

1. The comment was unkind. I responded to the comment.

_____

2. The disease is fatal. Maira is suffering from this disease.

_____

3. The bed was uncomfortable. I slept on it.

_____

4. That woman is beautiful. I am pointing at her.

_____

5. Tony is majoring in chemistry. My daughter is chatting with him.

_____

6. Those students are very hard working. I am proud of them.

_____

7. That diamond ring is beautiful. Samantha is looking at it.

_____

8. Alla is a teacher. Pietro is talking to her.

_____

9. The people are her close friends and family members. Sara depends on them.

_____

10. The compositions were written carelessly. The professor is dissatisfied with them.

Practice Writing

Use the following list to write sentences that contain adjective clauses that are the object of the preposition. The sentences can discuss your life, family, job, school or friends. Be certain to use the correct relative pronoun and to write sentences that exclude the relative pronoun, too.

e.g.   My cousin *with whom I am speaking* teaches in a college.

The employees *with whom my boss was satisfied* were given bonuses.

speak to	work with	wait for	prepare for
depend on	to be sure of	to be proud of	to take care of
believe in	compare to	to be ready for	to insist on
to be married to	to be engaged to	to be familiar with	to be satisfied with
to be miserable about	to be aware of	to be kind to	to be dissatisfied with
to listen to	to introduce to	to be kind to	to be responsible for
to hear about	to be different from	to be similar to	to be tired of

1. _____

2. _____

3. _____

4. _____

5. _____

Error Analysis

Read each of the following paragraphs, and correct any errors in the use of adjective clauses. When necessary merge sentences to prevent fragments and to make sentences richer.

1. Sofia to whom Marco is married. Sofia is very spoiled. Although she is thirty-four years old, she still wants her parents to solve all her problems. Now that Sofia has gotten married, her parents think her husband should work out all her issues quickly and quietly, as they have done for years. However, each month Sofia gets into more and more trouble. Last month she was fired from another job at which she had worked at it for less than three months. After losing this job, she went on a shopping spree during which she spent over $5,000. When she couldn't pay the bills, her father, with who Marco has had many disagreements, demanded Marco take a second job to support his daughter properly. What her parents don't realize is that Sofia who has the problem, not Marco who is struggling to make their lives work. I wonder what will happen in this relationship because there appears to be no solution.

2. Many foreign parents who I speak to. They believe that their children should follow their traditions strictly. For instance, some parents don't permit their children to date because dating which it is permitted in the United States is not part of their religious or cultural traditions to which these parents are accustomed to. Other parents who can't support themselves. They expect their children for whom they have made many sacrifices to finance them, even after the children get married and have families of their own. Many elderly immigrants can't imagine why their young people would want to follow American traditions, instead of the rich customs to which they have adhered to them for so many years.

Practice Writing

Select one of the following topics and write a letter. Include:

- an introduction paragraph that summarizes the problem problem;
- at least two body paragraphs that explain how to resolve this situation;
- a conclusion paragraph; and,
- be certain to include at least 5 adjective clauses to make your letter more interesting.

Topic One

Write a letter to the thirty-two year old woman who cannot meet a substantial man to explain how she can resolve her problem.

Topic Two

Write a letter to Marco explaining how he should handle Sofia and her parents.

Noun Clauses

In the previous chapters, you learned to form and use adverbial and adjectival dependent clauses. In this chapter, you will learn to create noun clauses, which can be used in place of a noun.

Read and respond to each question that follows.

What is a noun? A noun:

    a.   is the name of a person, place or thing.

    b.   describes or modifies an adverb.

    c.   refers to a noun

    d.   is the word that describes the action in a sentence.

Answer [1]

In the following chart, specify some examples of a noun as a person, place or thing.

	Person	Place	Thing or object
1.	President Bush	Central Park	the desk
2.			
3.			
4.			
5.			
6.			
7.			

---

[1] If you selected choice a, you are correct.

Read the following sentences, and circle all the nouns.

    a.   That college is located in Manhattan.

    b.   My dog was born in a small town in Germany.

    c.   The students sang a song about the holiday to the audience.

    d.   My aunt bought a big beautiful new car.

    e.   The class gave the instructor a gift.

Answer [2]

Read each of the following statements, and specify if it is true or false. If a statement is false, explain why.

	a.	When a noun is the subject of a sentence, it is placed after the verb.
	b.	When a noun is the object of a sentence, it is placed after the verb.
	c.	When a noun is the object of the preposition, it is placed before the preposition.
	d.	Prepositions are words such as in, on, above, to, from, etc.
	e.	The object of the preposition in the following sentence is word *door*. The child walked into the door.
	f.	A noun can be used as: the subject of a sentence; the object of a sentence; or as the object of a preposition.

Answers [3]

---

[2]   a.   That college is located in Manhattan.
    b.   My dog was born in a small town in Germany.
    c.   The students sang a song about the holiday to the audience.
    d.   My aunt bought a big beautiful new car.
    e.   The class gave the instructor a gift.
[3]   a.   False: when a noun is the subject of a sentence, it appears before the verb.
    b.   True
    c.   False: when a noun is the object of the preposition, it appears after the preposition
    d.   True
    e.   True
    f.   True

```
Nouns

A noun is the name of a person, place or thing.

        noun as
        subject         noun as        noun as
        ↓person        ↓a thing      ↓ a place
e.g.   Mary took a picture of Central Park.


A noun can function as the subject, object, and the object of the
preposition in a sentence.


          noun as              noun as       noun as object
          ↓subject             ↓object      ↓ of the preposition for
e.g.  The man bought a new car for his wife.
```

Underline the subject in each of the following sentences.

1. a. Her remark was true.

    b. What she said was true.

2. a. Miguel's behavior was inappropriate.

    b. What Miguel did was inappropriate.

3. a. Her demand was extremely unreasonable.

    b. What she demanded was extremely unreasonable.

Answer [4]

The difference between the subjects in letter a and letter b is:

    a. a simple noun is used in all the examples in letter a.

    b. in letter b instead of a noun, a noun clause is used.

    c. that letter b is grammatically incorrect.

    d. a and b

Answer [5]

---

[4] 1.   a. Her remark was true.
          b. What she said was true.
     2.   a. Miguel's behavior was inappropriate.
          b. What Miguel did was inappropriate.
     3.   a. Her demand was extremely unreasonable.
          b. What she demanded was extremely unreasonable.
[5] If you selected choice d, you are correct.

What is a noun clause? A noun clause is:

    a. an independent clause.

    b. a dependent clause that can take the place of an adjective.

    c. a dependent clause that can take the place of a noun.

    d. a noun clause can function as the subject of a sentence.

    e. c and d.

Answer [6]

Circle the noun clauses in the following sentence, and answer the questions that follow.

    a. Marta doesn't believe what Marco told her.

    b. Clarisa knows what she must do to pass.

    c. Bong realizes what he did wrong.

Answer [7]

In these sentences, the noun clause functions as:

    a. the subject of the sentence.

    b. the object of the sentence.

    c. the object of the preposition.

    d. an adjective.

Answer [8]

Circle the noun clauses in the following sentence, and answer the questions that follow.

    a. Mini doesn't know about what he said.

    b. Cara must be aware of what her son has done.

Answer [9]

In these two sets of sentences, the noun clause functions as _____

Answer [10]

---

[6] If you selected choice e, you are correct.

[7] a. Marta doesn't believe what Marco told her.

    b. Clarisa knows what she must do to pass.

    c. Bong Chul realizes what he did wrong.

[8] If you selected choice b, you are correct.

[9] a. Mini doesn't know about what he said.

    b. Cara must be aware of what her son has done.

[10] the object of the preposition.

Noun Clauses

A noun clause can be used in place of a noun. It can function as the subject, object or object of the preposition.

> **noun clause**
> ↓ **subject**
> e.g. *What Maria did* was terrible.

> **noun clause**
> ↓ **object**
> e.g. Anita told me *what he said to her.*

> ↓ **noun clause as the object**
> **of the preposition about**
> e.g. The child informed the police officer about *what he had seen.*

Forming Noun Clauses

The special word that begins a noun clause is called a _____ Answer [11]

Can a noun clause stand alone as a complete sentence? _____ Answer [12]

Can you write the general rule for creating a noun clause?

_____ + **subject** + _____ + (optional adjective, or object or prepositional phrase)

Answer [13]

Can you specify some of the relative pronouns used to begin noun clauses?

what _____ _____ _____ _____

_____ _____ _____ _____ _____

Answer [14]

---

[11] Relative pronoun
[12] No, a noun clause is not a sentences, but a dependent clause
[13] relative pronoun + subject + verb + (optional adjective, or object, or prepositional phrase)
[14] what, why, where, when, that, how, how much, how many, how long, how far, whether, whether or not, etc.

236

Read the following sentences, and note the rule for subject verb agreement when a noun clause is the subject of a sentence.

↓Noun clause   ↓verb
a. What we earn is not to be discussed.

↓Noun clause   ↓verb
b. How much a student learns in college depends on the student.

When a noun clause is the subject of the sentence, the verb must:

a. use the simple form (e.g. What we heard *be* private.)

b. use the third person singular: he, she or it. (e.g. What we heard *is* private.)

c. be eliminated from the sentence. (e.g. What we heard ~~is~~ private.)

d. none of these

Answer [15]

Do relative pronouns convey the same meaning as question words? _____ Answer [16]

What is done incorrectly in the noun clauses in the following sentences?

a. She doesn't know how long will she stay in this country.

b. What did she wrong is not a big deal.

In the above noun clauses, the writer:

a. did not make any mistakes.

b. confused the formation of a question with the formation of a noun clause.

c. used a noun clause as the object of the preposition.

d. all of these.

Answer [17]

Noun clauses are not questions, so that they are formed differently from questions.

---

[15] If you selected choice <u>b</u>, you are correct.

[16] No

[17] If you selected choice <u>b</u>, you are correct.

Forming Noun Clauses

A noun clause is formed by using the following rule.

relative pronoun + subject + verb + (optional object, adjective, or
prepositional phrase)

e.g. *What Maria said   Where I live   How much money I have*

**Noun clauses are *not* complete sentences, but dependent clauses that
must be connected to a main clause as follows.**

e.g.   ***What Maria said*** is untrue
I won't tell you ***where I live***
How much money I have is none of your business.

**When a noun clause is the subject of a sentence, the verb must agree
with the third person singular (he, she or it).**

e.g.   What Maria believes *is* questionable.
How long we will live here ***depends*** on our financial situation.

The following is a list of relative pronouns used to create noun clauses.

what	why	where	how much	how many	whether or not
whether	if	when	how far	how long	whatever

Controlled Practice

Noun Clauses as the Subject of the Sentence

With a partner or in a small group, read each question and write a response using the
noun clause as the subject of the sentence. Warning: a noun clause does not use the same
form as a question. In addition, be certain the main verb used after your noun clause is
written in the third person singular (he, she or it).

e.g.   How does Loretta earn a living?

How Loretta earns a living is a mystery to all of us.

How much does Eduardo owe the Internal Revenue Service?

How much money Eduardo owes the IRS depends on his income.

1. Why don't students proofread their compositions?

   _____

2. Where does our instructor live?

   _____

3. How many times did Mario fail chemistry?

   _____

4. How long has Cara been talking on the phone?

   _____

5. When does life begin?

   _____

Noun Clauses as the Object of the Sentence

With a partner or in a small group, read each question and write a response using a noun clause as the object of the sentence.

e.g.   How does Letizia get her homework done?

       I can't imagine *how Letizia gets her homework done.*

       When does Huang go school?

       I have no idea *when Huang goes to school.*

1. When will this semester end?

   _____

2. Why is the professor always late for class?

   _____

3. How far is it from New York to California?

   _____

4. How many more credits do you need to graduate?

_____

5. What gifts does Alana receive each year?

_____

Noun Clauses as the Object of the Preposition

With a partner, complete each of the following sentences by writing a noun clause that is the object of the preposition.

e.g.   The teacher talked about _____

The teacher talked about *what students must do to pass the courses.*

1. I am not crazy about _____.

2. That man must learn to cope with _____.

3. We don't agree with _____.

4. The bank manager will take care of _____.

5. They have expressed their feelings about _____.

Practice Writing

Write a paragraph about your best friend, your parents, neighbors, co-workers or classmates describing what you have done, said or discussed with them recently.

e.g. On the first day of class, my chemistry teacher explained *what the students are required to do during labs and for homework.* He told us *how many exams we would have.* He also explained *how many absences we were permitted.*

Using Noun Clauses to Modify a Noun or an Adjective

Read the following sentences. Place the letter *S* above the subject, the letter *V* above the verb, and circle the noun clause.

The reasons why I disagree are clear.

The fact that a student has missed ten classes is a valid reason to fail.

The times when I arrived late were recorded by the professor.[18]

In these three examples, the noun clauses _____,

   a. modify the main verb in the sentence.

   b. modify the noun, which is the subject.

   c. modify the object if of the sentence.

   d. none of these

Answer [19]

Read the following sentences. Place the letter *S* above the subject, the letter *V* above the verb, the letters *ADJ* above the adjective, and circle the noun clauses.

I was afraid that we were lost.

She was certain that she would fail the course again.

They were delighted when they heard the news about the new baby.

Answer [20]

---

[18]
$\quad$ S $\qquad\qquad$ V
The reasons why I disagree are clear.
$\quad$ S $\qquad\qquad\qquad\qquad$ V
The fact that a student has missed ten classes is a valid reason to fail.
$\quad$ S $\qquad\qquad$ V
The times when I arrived late were recorded by the professor.

[19] If you selected choice b, you are correct.

[20] S V ADJ
I was afraid that we were lost.
S V ADJ
She was certain that she would fail the course again.
S V ADJ
They were delighted when they heard the news about the new baby.

In these three examples, the noun clause _____,

    a. modifies the verb

    b. modifies the subject

    c. modifies the adjective

    d. none of these

Answer [21]

Noun clause can:

    a. be the subject of a sentence.

    b. be the object of the sentence or the object of the preposition.

    c. modify a noun.

    d. modify an adjective.

    e. all of these

Answer [22]

More Uses of Noun Clauses

A noun clause can modify a noun.

                noun clause
      ↓ subject ↓modifies a noun   ↓verb
e.g. The reason *why Marna lied to me* was obvious.

A noun clause can also modify an adjective.

                 noun clause
        adjective↓ ↓modifies an adjective
e.g. Anita was very happy *that he visited her.*

Controlled Practice

With a partner or in a small group, complete each sentence with a noun clause that either modifies the adjective or the noun specified.

e.g.   I was dissatisfied _____.

        I was dissatisfied *that Loretta didn't pay her bill on time.*

---

[21] If you selected choice c, you are correct.
[22] If you selected choice e, you are correct.

1. The child was frightened _____.

2. The reason _____ was stated in her

   letter.

3. The time _____ was not humorous.

4. The child was happy _____.

5. I was concerned_____.

6. The fact _____ is well known.

7. The explanation _____ was specified in the rejection

   letter that the college had sent her.

8. The reason _____ was unclear.

9. The teachers were unaware _____.

10. It was obvious _____.

Noun Clauses and the Subjunctive Mood

Read the following sentences, and circle the noun clauses.

   a. We demanded that he <u>see</u> a doctor.

   b. The lawyer recommended that the woman <u>take</u> an insurance policy.

   c. It is critical that the baby <u>get</u> immunized against certain diseases.

Answer [23]

---

[23] a. We demanded that he see a doctor.
   b. The lawyer recommended that the woman take an insurance policy.
   c. It is critical that the baby get immunized against certain diseases.

In these noun clauses, the verb doesn't follow the rules of present tense subject verb agreement because:

a. the present tense is rarely used in noun clauses.

b. the verb in the main clause stresses the importance of a situation, and therefore must use the subjunctive mood.

c. the rules of subject verb agreement don't apply to noun clauses.

d. all of these.

Answer [24]

Read the following sentences and circle the noun clauses.

a. We demanded that he <u>not see</u> that psychic anymore.

b. The doctor insisted that the woman <u>not take</u> the medicine.

c. It is critical that the baby <u>not get</u> exposed to dangerous childhood diseases.

Answer [25]

Noun clauses in the subjunctive mood are made negative by:

a. inserting the word *not* after the verb. (e.g. We insisted she *see not* that man.)

b. inserting the word *not* before the verb. (e.g. We insisted she *not see* that man.)

c. inserting the auxiliary verb do/does plus the word *not* before the verb. (We insisted she *does not see* that man.)

d. none of these.

Answer [26]

---

[24] If you selected choice <u>b</u>, you are correct.

[25] a. We demanded that he <u>not see</u> the psychic anymore.

b. The doctor insisted that the woman <u>not take</u> the medicine.

c. It is critical that the baby <u>not get</u> exposed to dangerous childhood diseases.

[26] If you selected choice <u>b</u>, you are correct.

Noun Clauses and the Subjunctive Mood

When a noun clause expresses the importance of a situation, the verb in the noun clauses uses the simple form as follows.

↓verb
stresses
importance

↓simple
form of
verb

e.g. She requested that he *call* her immediately.

When a noun clause is negative and expresses the importance of a situation, the noun clause is formed by placing the word *not* after the subject and before the verb as follows

e.g.   I insisted **that he *not call* me** anymore.

When the following verbs are followed by a noun clause, use the subjunctive mood as discussed above.

insist	demand	request	be important
be crucial advise	suggest	be critical	
recommend	be essential	propose	be imperative

Controlled Practice:

Complete each of the following sentences with a noun clause, where the word *not* is indicated make the noun clause negative.

e.g.   The doctor insisted that my father _____.

The doctor insisted that my father *go on a diet.*

The professor said it is important that students (not) _____

The professor said it is important that students *not be late or absent.*

1. It is critical that the child _____.

2. The professor recommends that each student _____.

3. The union proposes that each employee _____.

4. It is essential that you (not) _____.

5. The letter requests that her boyfriend (not) _____.

6. I suggest that Marina _____.

7. The child always demands that his mother _____.

8. It is crucial that Sven (not) _____.

9. I always emphasize that students _____.

10. His parents stress that their son _____.

Contextualized Practice

With a partner, read the following letter, and complete each blank with a noun clause, using the rules you just learned in this chapter.

Dear Elena:

I am writing to ask your advise about a problem that I am having with a classmate who used to be my friend.

This semester I enrolled in a writing class with Alicia because I didn't want to be in a class where I didn't know anyone. At first, everything was great. Alicia and I sat next to each other, shared notes and even helped one another with assignments. However, as the semester progressed, I met some new friends whom Alicia immediately disliked. Although I realized _____ , I didn't think she had the right to tell me with whom I could associate. Consequently, I continued to be friendly with the other students until she finally demanded that I _____.

When I refused to acquiesce, Alicia became extremely angry and started to malign (bad mouth) me in front of these people. Now much to my surprise, she has convinced my new friends _____ and that they should avoid me if they don't want to be harassed by me. I was shocked

_____ , so I approached Alicia before class and asked her to

246

stop lying about me. As soon as she was in earshot of these people, she began to scream and accused me of _____.

Now all these people think _____, even though it is Alicia who is lying and harassing me, but the worst part is that my classmates think that _____. I don't know _____, so I thought that I would ask you for suggestions.

Marlena

Practice Writing

Topic One:

Write a letter to Marlena to tell her what you think she should do about her problem. Be certain to write and underline at least six (6) noun clauses using the rules you just learned.

Topic Two

Write a composition describing a time when you had difficulty with a classmate, teacher, employer, neighbor or friend. Be certain to include and underline least six (6) noun clauses that use the rules you just learned.

Simple form of verb	Simple Present Tense	Simple Past Tense	Past Participle
be	am/is/are	was, were	been
become		became	become
begin		began	begun
bend		bent	bent
bite		bit	bitten
blow		blew	blown
break		broke	broken
bring		brought	brought
build		built	built
buy		bought	bought
catch		caught	caught
choose		chose	chosen
cling		clung	clung
come		came	come
cost		cost	cost
cut		cut	cut
dig		dug	dug
do	do/does	did	done
draw		drew	drawn
drink		drank	drunk
drive		drove	driven
eat		ate	eaten
fall		fell	fallen
feed		fed	fed
feel		felt	felt
fight		fought	fought
find		found	found
flee		fled	fled
fling		flung	flung
fly		flew	flown

Simple Form of Verb	Simple Present Tense	Simple Past Tense	Past Participle
forbid		forbade	forbidden
forget		forgot	forgotten
forgive		forgave	forgiven
freeze		froze	frozen
get		got	gotten
give		gave	given
go	go/goes	went	gone
grind		ground	ground
grow		grew	grown
hang		hung	hung
have	has/have	had	had
hear		heard	heard
hide		hid	hidden
hit		hit	hit
hold		held	held
hurt		hurt	hurt
keep		kept	kept
kneel		knelt	knelt
know		knew	known
lay		laid	laid
lead		led	led
leap		leapt	leapt
leave		left	left
lend		lent	lent
let		let	let
lie		lay	lain
light		lit	lit
lose		lost	lost
make		made	made
mean		meant	meant

Simple Form of Verb	Simple Present Tense	Simple Past Tense	Past Participle
meet		met	met
pay		paid	paid
prove		proved	proved/proven
put		put	put
quit		quit	quit
read		read	read
ride		rode	ridden
ring		rang	rung
rise		rose	risen
run		ran	run
say		said	said
see		saw	seen
seek		sought	sought
sell		sold	sold
send		sent	sent
set		set	set
sew		sewed	sewn/sewed
shake		shook	shaken
shoot		shot	shot
shut		shut	shut
smg		sang	sung
sit		sat	sat
sleep		slept	slept
slide		slid	slid
speak		spoke	spoken
speed		sped	sped
spend		spent	spent
spill		spilt	spilt
stand		stood	stood
steal		stole	stolen

Simple Form of Verb	Simple Present Tense	Simple Past Tense	Past Participle
stick		stuck	stuck
strike		struck	stricken
swear		swore	sworn
sweep		swept	swept
swim		swam	swum
take		took	taken
teach		taught	taught
tear		tore	torn
tell		told	told
think		thought	thought
throw		threw	thrown
understand		understood	understood
wake		woke	woken
wear		wore	worn
weave		wove	woven
win		won	won
wind		wound	wound
withdraw		withdrew	withdrawn
write		wrote	written